Karl Ludvigsen was born in Kalamazoo, Michigan, and attended both M.I.T. and Pratt Institute. Since 1967 Mr. Ludvigsen has been working full-time as an automotive author and free-lance journalist. He is presently east coast editor of *Motor Trend* and a contributing editor of *Signature*, and has also served in editorial capacities for *Automobile Quarterly, Car and Driver* and *Sports Cars Illustrated*. His other books include *Guide to Corvette Speed, Inside Story of the Fastest Fords, Group 7, Corvette, The Mercedes-Benz Racing Cars* and *Wankel Engines A to Z*.

Mr. Ludvigsen also has an extensive background within the automotive industry. During 1956 he worked as a designer on General Motors' styling staff and from 1961 through 1966 he worked both in Detroit and New York on the GM news relations team.

Karl Ludvigsen was founder and first president of the Motor Racing Safety Society. He is also a member of the Guild of Motoring Writers, the Society of Automotive Engineers, the Society of Automotive Historians, the International Motor Press Association and the American Society of Journalists and Authors.

From 1971 through 1974 he had been honored by the American Auto Racing Writers and Broadcasters Association for his technical and feature writing. Other awards include the Montagu Trophy, awarded by the Guild of Motoring Writers; the Cugnot Award, bestowed by the Society of Automotive Historians; and the Ken W. Purdy Award from the International Motor Press Association.

Mr. Ludvigsen resides in Pelham Manor, New York, where he is constantly at work on new automotive books and articles. He closely followed Dan Gurney's rise to prominence as one of America's top racing drivers and the emergence and achievements of All American Racers, Inc. — creators of Gurney's Eagles.

Cover painting and illustration of author by Mike Patrick, Minneapolis. Book and cover design by William F. Kosfeld.

This inscribed photo of Dan Gurney was sent to new members of the AAR Eagle Club, formed so that enthusiasts could support AAR through small contributions.

Karl Ludvigsen

GURNEY'S EAGLES

The Exciting Story of the AAR Racing Cars

Motorbooks International
Publishers & Wholesalers ®

*To Aari and Miles
from their father
with love.*

First published in 1992 by Motorbooks International Publishers &
Wholesalers, PO Box 2, 729 Prospect Avenue, Osceola, WI 54020
USA

This new edition is a facsimile of the original 1976 edition with
updated corrections and revisions added

The information in this book is true and complete to the best of our
knowledge. All recommendations are made without any guarantee
on the part of the author or Publisher, who also disclaim any liability
incurred in connection with the use of this data or specific details

We recognize that some words, model names and designations, for
example, mentioned herein are the property of the trademark holder.
We use them for identification purposes only. This is not an official
publication

Motorbooks International books are also available at discounts in
bulk quantity for industrial or sales-promotional use. For details write
to Special Sales Manager at the Publisher's address

Library of Congress Cataloging-in-Publication Data
Ludvigsen, Karl E.
  Gurney's Eagles: the exciting story of the AAR racing cars /
Karl Ludvigsen.—[2nd ed.]
     p. cm.
  Includes bibliographical references and index.
  ISBN 0-87938-651-7
  1. Automobiles, Racing—United States—History. 2. Grand
Prix racing. 3. Gurney, Dan. I. Title.
TL236.L8 1992
629.228—dc20   92-1265

Printed and bound in the United States of America

FOREWORD

I would like to take this opportunity to thank Karl for the effort and determination he has shown in putting together this fine book. All of us at AAR are honored and thrilled that he has done it. I am also thankful that this is a difficult book to compose an ending for. . . . In other words, we are still going strong!

My memories of the years since 1964 are blurred slightly, so it has been a great thrill for me to relive those days. I suppose I could be pardoned if I said, "Wow! Did we do all that?"

I'm also happy that our major sponsors, such as the Goodyear Tire and Rubber Company, the Earle M. Jorgensen Steel Company, and Ozzie Olson and his Olsonite Corporation, have been mentioned. There have been many others, such as Castrol, Mobil, Valvoline, STP, Bardahl, Union 76, RAC Instruments, IZOD Clothing, Yamaha, Champion Spark Plugs and the Ford Motor Company, who have given us real financial support in the form of hard cash plus products, and we are very thankful to them. But without the first three — Goodyear, Jorgensen and Olsonite — there would have been no story.

As the reader will see, much of our effort has been in the form of a search for the elusive 'magic speed secret' that boils down to that much-used but little-understood term, 'vehicle dynamics.' This search has tried the patience of us all. It has also caused irreparable damage to delicate human relationships as we put our expertise, or lack of it, on the line in front of the world at each race. That there have been ego problems is no surprise, since we are all human. Many of those who are no longer with us deserve a good share of the credit for our achievements.

Yes, Karl, you have managed to rattle some of the skeletons in my closet full of memories of the old feuds I had (maybe still have. . . . Ha! Ha!) with the great auto racing press.

I suppose all of us want a niche in history, provided, of course, it is a good one. With this book, you have made me, my family and all of us at AAR very proud. We are also looking to the future so that you may write an equally entertaining sequel in 1986.

Happy new decade,

Dan Gurney
Santa Ana, California
January, 1976

PREFACE

Many traditions evolved during the first fifty years of road racing. One of the strongest held that the worlds of the builders and the drivers were completely separate. The engineers created the cars; the drivers were simply to step in and take the controls; and the poor team manager had to preserve peace between them, for the drivers were seen by the designers as boorish louts more likely than not to destroy their precious creations by mishandling them.

During the fifties an erosion of this tradition began. Those who broke with it were viewed at first as the exceptions that proved the rule: Stirling Moss of England, who many felt would have had greater success if he had stopped experimenting with his cars; Jack Brabham, who came into racing as much as a builder as a driver (but then he was, after all, an Australian, and so was pardoned his eccentricity); Jean Behra of France, who had gained much of his technical skill as a motorcycle racer.

These men were in the vanguard of a movement that established a new tradition in the sixties: That of the successful driver-builder. It came about for several reasons. One was that the rise of independent makers of racing engines and transmissions made it easier to put a racing car together. Another was that closer communication between the driver and his car and crew was becoming more important to success, as knowledge of handling and chassis-tuning grew. Yet another reason was the ability of the driver-builder to share more fully in the financial benefits of road racing. Among the drivers who set up car companies during this period were Jim Hall, Bruce McLaren, Jack Brabham, John Surtees and California's own Dan Gurney.

From the beginning of his career behind the wheel Dan Gurney believed in using his mechanical knowledge and instincts to gain an advantage on the race track. His early associations were with men like Jerry Eisert, Bill Fowler, Frank Arciero, Max Balchowsky and Mickey Thompson, for whom the most exotic creation of a foreign race car builder was mere raw material, susceptible to infinite improvement. While driving cars they owned or prepared, Gurney began absorbing knowledge about what makes a machine go fast and finish fast.

When Dan started to apply that knowledge he often broke with precedent by lifting the front or rear hood and working on the car himself. Eager to make a change that he felt might help him and the car lap faster, he didn't wait to see if he could persuade a team manager to ask a mechanic to do it. We journalists saw this, and because Dan's last-minute adjustments were sometimes followed by a poor performance, we labeled him a 'tinkerer' whose experiments were likely to foul up a perfectly good automobile. In retrospect, I think we were wrong to do so.

Why do I think that? Because we now know that on many such occasions Gurney was striving to breathe life into a machine that he knew was terminally ill before it left the starting grid. Because Dan's record as a driver and builder proves that he knew what he was doing. And because Dan says so. He admits that not all his adjustments have worked, but adds, "I would say that I was successful at least nine out of ten times." Even the failures were fodder for future tests that would be more productive.

Even if we had fully appreciated what Dan Gurney was doing when he was doing it, I doubt that we'd have predicted that he would become the most important American builder of racing cars in the rear-engine era. We might have guessed if we'd paid attention on such occasions as his first month of May at Indianapolis in 1962. Dan passed his rookie test in an Offy-powered roadster. Then he practiced in the first turbine-powered car ever to be officially entered at the Speedway. He was the only qualifier to drive a mid-engined car with a stock-block engine, and by personally inviting Colin Chapman of Lotus to Indianapolis on race day he changed the whole course of racing history.

It's been my pleasure to record some of that history as Dan Gurney and the AAR Eagles have made it. Writing it wasn't made any easier by my recollection that Dan once expressed a low opinion of automotive journalists (even though he married one!). In spite of that — or because of it — Dan was willing to review this manuscript and offer suggestions for its improvement. I owe him warm thanks for that as well as for many conversations over the AAR years that have helped me understand why the Eagles are as they are. Any errors, however, are my responsibility alone.

I am also indebted to Evi Butz Gurney, Don Markland, John Miller, Gary Wheeler, Bill Fowler and Susie Breidenbach of All American Racers for specific information about the Eagles. Former AAR employees who have been generous with their time and thoughts are Max Muhleman, Bill Dunne and Roman Slobodynskyj. Much-needed photographs were rounded up by Pete Biro, James P. Chapman and Oscar L. 'Ozzie' Olson. Other photos are from the author's collection, which includes prints from the AAR archives and from photographer Stanley Rosenthall. Thanks are due also to William Kosfeld, Mary Calby and Sharin Henricks of Motorbooks International for their thoughtful and meticulous editorial attention.

Finally, I offer thanks to Dan Gurney for the Foreword, and also for the lifetime he has given so unselfishly to the sport of motor racing. In his five years as a builder alone, Gurney has competed with the same intensity he showed in sixteen years as a driver. Thank you, too, Dan, on behalf of all racing enthusiasts, for creating the AAR Eagle, the car whose shriek was heard 'round the racing world.

Karl Ludvigsen
Pelham Manor, New York
March, 1976

CONTENTS

AAR and Indy

Like many marriages that traced their beginnings to a liaison in the sober luxury of a London taxi, this one did not last. This was of little account, for the union itself was of less import than the offspring it spawned: the extraordinary Eagle cars. Winners in Formula 1, USAC and SCCA competition, the American Eagles have written a chapter of their own in the modern history of racing cars. They've come to stand for elegant design and for precision and uniformity of manufacture. Some of the handsomest cars ever to take to the track have been Eagles. And they were the creations of one of the most intensely dedicated teams in racing.

That meeting of minds during a London cab ride took place late in 1962. The occasion marked the first time that two of America's finest racing drivers realized they had a common dream: the construction of an internationally top-ranked racing car in the United States. One driver was Daniel Gurney, tall, blond Californian, fresh from a season in which he won his first Grand Prix with Porsche and had his first tantalizing taste of Indianapolis. The other was Carroll Shelby, tall, dark Texan, who was just getting his AC Cobra production going a year and a half after his retirement from competitive driving.

Gurney and Carroll Shelby at Watkins Glen.

Dan went on to race three Grand Prix seasons for Jack Brabham, and it was during the second of these, in 1964, that he took the first of the several steps that were to lead to the Eagles. In California he set up a small racing team of his own. His first employee was Bill Fowler, who had attended to the Ferraris and Lotuses Gurney had driven for Frank Arciero and who had also been chief mechanic to Dan's Indy Lotus in 1963. Aided by machinist Ken Deringer, Fowler extensively modified and Ford-powered a Lotus 19B, which Gurney drove to second place in the fall professional race at Laguna Seca and then took to early leads (before retiring) at Daytona and Sebring in February and March of 1965.

These were the fledgling wing-flutters of the bird that would become the Eagle. They were nurtured by Carroll Shelby, wise in the politics of racing, who knew how desperately Goodyear yearned to wrest from Firestone its historic domination of America's premier event, the Indianapolis 500. He helped Gurney win substantial backing from Goodyear — the aim being an Indy victory — and in return he was granted a half interest in the Gurney racing company.

During the negotiations with Goodyear, Dan was asked what he intended to call his company. Before he had a chance to reply, Goodyear president Victor Holt suggested "All American Racers." He thought of it in the context that the term 'all-American' enjoys in football; that is, a team chosen from the best America has to offer. "He mentioned the name," Dan later told interviewer Peter Manso, "and while it didn't appeal to me at the time, it was done in such a way that we felt obligated to say, 'Yes, that's a great name and that's what it will be,' and so that's the way it was named."[1]

All three of AAR's first Indy entries, a Lotus and two Halibrand Shrikes, retired in the 1965 500, but Joe Leonard did collect an AAR victory in a Shrike in the Milwaukee 200 that year. In the meantime a permanent home for All American Racers, Inc., was rising on a one-acre corner lot in Santa Ana, south of Los Angeles: a single-story building with no exterior identification, its 16,000 square feet of floor area ideally arranged for the designing, building, preparing and selling of racing cars and engines. By the end of September, 1965, the facility was ready and the making of Eagles could begin.

To design his cars Gurney hired the Briton, Len Terry, whom he'd come to know during the joint struggle of Lotus and Ford to win at Indianapolis. Terry had done the special 19B Lotus sports car to Dan's order in 1964 and, as Lotus chief designer, was responsible for the sleek Type 38 Lotus-Ford with which Jim Clark finally won the Indy 500 in 1965. Right

[1] Peter Manso, *Vrooom!!* (New York: Funk & Wagnalls, 1969), p. 30.

after that race Terry joined AAR. In September he was followed by John Lambert, a former Lotus associate, who took charge of getting the cars built. From the Brabham organization Gurney lured Peter Wilkins, an Australian with a genius for welding and shaping metal.

Another on the twenty-two-man AAR strength at the end of 1965 was engine wizard John Miller, whose modest anonymity inspired one of the memorable T-shirt captions of American racing: "Who the hell is John Miller?" An AAR stalwart since January, 1965, Miller's background in

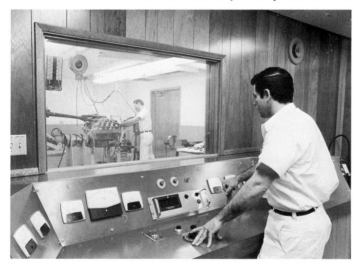 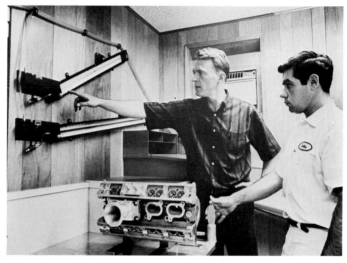

motorcycle tuning helped him extract peak power from the Eagle engines. In April of '65 Wayne Leary joined AAR as a mechanic for driver Roger McCluskey and stayed with the Gurney gang to become chief mechanic — 'crew chief' in Gasoline Alley jargon — for AAR's Indianapolis entries. Leary, a quiet, intense perfectionist, would give much of the credit for his success to such capable assistants as Dean Williams and Butch Wilson.

This was part of the 'all-American' crew that had been assembled with the help of Goodyear dollars (in excess of one million) to assure a

Left: John Miller at the AAR dyno controls with an Indy four-cam Ford V-8 on the bench. Right: Gurney and Miller check data on airflow testing of an Indy Ford engine inlet port.

victory in Indiana. They knew what tires they'd be using, and what engine: The four-cam 4.2-liter American Ford V-8 had proved its superiority to the unblown Offy — in the right chassis — at the Speedway in 1965. There was Ford spirit at AAR anyway, born on the western dry lakes where Gurney and Fowler once raced flat-head Ford V-8's. With his own special slide-throttle inlet setup, John Miller had tweaked the Ford-built Indy engine to a healthy 575 bhp without nitro. All that remained was to decide what kind of car to wrap around it.

Gurney also planned to build an AAR Formula 1 car (see Chapter 2), and it was his aim to tailor each auto precisely to its job. In fact one original plan had been to name the Indy cars 'Gurneys' and the Grand Prix cars 'Eagles.' But the designs became similar and the names identical. There had been at least eight Eagle marques before, two in Britain and the rest in the U.S. (plus Adler in Germany), but none could claim the fame that would accrue to the AAR Eagles. Their handsome emblem, an Eagle's head surrounded by the letter G, was the work of Dan's father. And the suggestion of an Eagle's beak in the contour of the radiator air inlet was one of the most successful design motifs ever applied to any car, racing or otherwise.

Early in 1966: preparation of jigs and pieces for the first Eagle monocoques at the new AAR factory.

From the beak to the back the Indy Eagle of 1966 bore an unsurprising resemblance to the Lotus 38. Len Terry alone did all the drawings for it in five months, starting in September, 1965, and it differed from the successful '65 Lotus only where it needed to. There wasn't time to innovate since the aim was to build not one or two but six cars in time for the race in May, 1966. Thus a kinship with the Lotus 38 in all main design features was undeniable.

The main structure was a true tubular monocoque body/frame made of 2024 and 5052 grades of aluminum alloy sheet, with an outer skin thickness of 16 swg. Boxes formed by the flanks of the frame added torsional stiffness (excellent at 6,000 lb.-ft./degree without the engine) and contained the bladder fuel tanks. These were scanty at sixty-five U.S. gallons; for the Indy race most of the cars had extra tanks strapped on their left sides to bring the capacity close to the legal maximum of seventy-five U.S. gallons. Rearward extensions of the frame carried the engine and were joined by a ring bulkhead that encircled the Hewland two-speed transaxle and also provided suspension mounting points. Twin bulkheads at the front supported the suspension plus the pedal assembly, oil tank and radiator.

The front and rear suspensions were of the classical format established on earlier Lotuses, with rocker-type upper front wishbones operating inboard-mounted springs, shock absorbers and an anti-roll bar. The Eagle differed from the Lotus 38 in many details, however. Instead of having the body offset three inches to the left on the track of the car, as the Lotus 38 did, the Eagle sat symmetrically on its wheels. Its builders felt that the penalties of offset suspension — tendencies to swerve to the right on braking and to the left on acceleration — weren't acceptable in exchange for a slight increase in cornering power.

"In designing their suspension and other tubular components," wrote Len Terry, "I went up in diameter and down in wall thickness wherever possible (in comparison with the Lotus 38) to gain strength without weight penalty. I used live stub-axles at the front for the first time, since these could be made lighter and more rigid than the dead type. Front and rear suspension systems were similar to those of the Lotus but with anti-dive inclination of the wishbone pivots at the front."[2] The pivot axis of the upper wishbone was level, while that of the lower one was inclined upward toward the rear to give the convergence of the axes that provided an anti-dive moment. This feature would not survive the early tests of the Eagle.

Another technique Terry carried over from the Lotus 38 was a simple system that automatically replenished the nose oil tank from an auxiliary tank placed above the driver's legs. All the new Indy Eagles had full rounded tails and some degree of covering for the Ford engine, and some of the cars, those of Lloyd Ruby and Roger McCluskey, had close-fitting jackets for the air inlet stacks. The specially-designed six-spoke magnesium wheels were exceedingly good-looking and became a hallmark of the Eagle car.

According to the date stamped on its dash plate, the first Indy Eagle monocoque was completed on February 11, 1966. And its first test runs took place four weeks later, on Sunday, March 13, running the 'wrong way' on the 2.7-mile road course at Riverside. Gurney turned thirty-five laps with his new creation and then gave it to Jerry Grant for a few additional laps. Publicly Dan expressed pleasure with the first Eagle, but privately he was alarmed by the car's instability on the straight at Riverside. It "gave me gray hairs," he said later. Dan traced the cause to the front suspension's anti-dive geometry, which produced a changing castor angle with wheel travel, and he had the lower wishbone pivots set level to remove that effect. This change, which solved the problem, was vociferously opposed by Len Terry and caused a sharp deterioration in the working relationship between Gurney and Terry.

On April 22, as the AAR preparations for Indy were getting up to speed, all security restrictions were removed from the Eagle's natal phase. The public learned that Bardahl and Yamaha would be additional sponsors for the 1966 program. In May, five Ford-powered Eagles were ready to race at Indy, and all five made the starting field. Gurney was shooting for the pole during qualifying, or at least the front row, so John Miller had his engine humming nicely. The only problem was that the

[2]Len Terry and Alan Baker, *Racing Car Design and Development* (Cambridge, Massachusetts: Robert Bentley, 1973), pp 56-57.

clutch couldn't handle the power, with the result that each of the three qualifying attempts Dan made on the first day ended in clutch failure. On the second day he made the race with a speed of 160.499 mph, which placed him in the seventh row. If he'd turned the same speed on the first day he would have been in the third row, which, as it turned out, would have been much better.

The fastest Eagle qualifier was Lloyd Ruby with 162.433 mph in his AAR-entered Bardahl Eagle, and Jerry Grant had tenth spot on the grid with a privately entered car. Gurney, Leonard and McCluskey were in a clump in nineteenth through twenty-first starting positions. This was the

Indy, 1966: Note the supplemental left-hand fuel tank. USAC rules caused AAR to designate the 'tail feathers' as exhaust pipe braces. They helped in the same way a small wing would, something the competition didn't realize.

Lloyd Ruby's Eagle on its way to eleventh place at Indy in 1966.

Cockpit of Joe Leonard's Eagle at Indy in 1966. The steering wheel is cut away for leg clearance.

Jerry Grant and his retired Eagle-Ford at Trenton, 1966.

wrong place to be, it developed, for there was a colossal multiple crash at the end of the main straight, right at the fall of the starting flag. It sheared the left wheels off Dan's car and forced Joe Leonard to flat-spot all his tires. All the Eagles but Dan's were able to restart, whereupon the phlegmatic Ruby went for first place and claimed it at the 175-mile mark. He held off challenges from Jim Clark and Jackie Stewart but had to give up the lead 200 miles later when his engine forced him to make a long pit stop. Not one Eagle was running at the finish; Leonard, Grant, Ruby and McCluskey were awarded ninth, tenth, eleventh and thirteenth places on the basis of the number of laps they completed.

The Eagle was beautiful, but could it bite? There was reason to wonder after this traumatic debut. Its first victory finally came on August 7 on the historic mile track at Langhorne, Pennsylvania, over 150 miles in the hands of Roger McCluskey. In the following month Len Terry left the services of AAR and Dan Gurney, with whom he had not been getting on too well, and the following year co-founder Carroll Shelby sold his share of AAR to Gurney; Shelby would chase the chimera of a turbine car of his own for Indy. These events made it crystal clear that in the future AAR would rise or fall solely on the talents — of administration, of engineering and of race-driving — of Daniel Sexton Gurney. He would have help, of course: In the years ahead ex-publicist Max Muhleman would serve as the AAR general manager, for example. But there was never any suggestion that he was more than an able spokesman for Gurney.

For the 1967 USAC season AAR laid down seven new cars much like the Eagles of 1966, cars that had been too new the year before to have

Indy, 1967: Dan (left) and Jerry Grant (right) return to the track after pit stops. The slight, one-inch offset is visible.

John Miller checks the cockpit of Gurney's car prior to the 1967 500.

The Mark III Gurney Weslake 305-cid Ford engine in Rindt's Eagle.

Jochen Rindt's Eagle begins its terminal smoking spell at Indy in 1967.

a chance to show to best advantage. At Indianapolis Gurney tested features of the '67 car before the Speedway closed at the end of 1966, winning some buyers for his new model by turning tire-testing laps at better than 166 mph. Changes included a modest one-inch, left-hand offset of the fuselage, accomplished by altering suspension parts, and the integration into the main shell of the added fuel capacity on the left-hand side.

Five of the new Eagles qualified in the 1967 field, Dan Gurney's placing in the first row with a second-fastest 167.224 mph four-lap average. And through the quarter-distance mark of the race, Dan 'led his

Gurney with Grand Prix and Indy ace
Jim Clark, at Indy in 1967.

class,' first among the piston-engined cars but second behind the formidable STP-Paxton turbine car driven by Parnelli Jones. Then, however, he made a prolonged pit stop: "I was forced to stop when my fuel tank selector valve refused to work. This meant that although I had half my fuel load remaining, it was in the left-hand tanks and the jammed valve wouldn't permit me to switch over. I actually ran out of fuel, which caused the engine to run lean and burn several valves. That immediately cost me a couple of cylinders and later forced me out altogether." Indeed, only one of the seven Eagle-Fords in the field was running at the flag: Denny Hulme's car, prepared by Smokey Yunick.

Left: Denny Hulme took fourth place at Indy in 1967—highest-placed Eagle and the only one running at the finish. Right: Bobby Unser received ninth place money in a car owned by Bob Wilke—beginning of the long association between Bobby Unser and Eagles.

Goodyear got the Indy victory it craved in 1967; Foyt's Coyote-Ford provided it. Later in '67 A.J. Foyt used an Eagle for some of the miles he drove toward his fifth USAC National Driving Championship. At Riverside, on November 26, Gurney scored his first personal USAC Eagle victory in the Rex Mays 300. Two aspects of this victory were significant. One was that Dan was sponsored, for the first time, by Oscar L. 'Ozzie' Olson of Detroit. After a brief conversation and a handshake between Dan and Ozzie, Dan's car became the Olsonite Eagle, the first of many AAR-birds to bear that name. Olson, a successful maker of steering wheels and toilet seats, remained a major Eagle backer through 1974. The other significant

Gurney stops for fuel and tires en route to victory in the 1967 Rex Mays 300 at Riverside. Engine is a Mark IV Gurney Weslake/Ford.

Dan and his sponsor, Ozzie Olson (with champagne) enjoy the 1967 Riverside win, the first of two Rex Mays 300 victories.

aspect of the Riverside win was that the Eagle was powered by an engine of Gurney's own design and construction.

This Ford-based engine was at the American end of the axis of co-operation between AAR and British engine tuning genius Harry Weslake. It came into being because the internationalistic Gurney had been impressed by the levels of specific power being extracted in England from humble Ford fours for Formulas 2 and Junior. "Why not try to do something similar with the Ford Fairlane V-8?" reasoned Gurney. He sketched out his ideas for changes to the 289-cid Fairlane and presented them to the Weslake group at Rye, in southern England, asking whether they could help him with the modifications. They agreed to do so.

Harry Weslake and his staff prepared drawings for new aluminum cylinder heads to fit the American Ford engine. They had circular inlet ports, valves inclined at nine degrees to the cylinder centerline instead of the stock twenty degrees, and combustion chambers with the heart-shaped outline that was a Weslake trademark. Under John Miller's supervision the first such heads were cast in the United States by Alcoa, and then two more sets of heads, a Mark II version, were made in England for AAR by Weslake. Though Weslake had initiated the design, to Gurney's requirements, virtually all the development and testing were done in Santa Ana by John Miller.

In 1966 a Mark III Gurney Weslake head was built, improved in its structure and its ease of assembly. At the end of that year it was first tested with fuel injection and alcohol blends and fitted into an Eagle chassis: the car Dan had driven so briefly at Indy in 1966. This was brought to the Speedway again in 1967, and it just squeaked into the field in the hands of Jochen Rindt. It was the only stock-based engine (allowed 305 cubic inches of displacement) to race at Indianapolis that year. Rindt brought it up to sixteenth place but with three-fourths of the distance still to go it began smoking from broken piston rings (a chronic early problem with this engine) and retired after running 108 of the 200 laps.

Late in 1966 AAR started work on a lighter and less bulky Mark IV edition of the heads, identifiable by their narrower rocker covers and the inward inclination of their carburetors or inlet ram pipes. Intended to be

Fairlane, four-cam and Mark III Gurney Weslake/Ford engines being prepared in AAR's 'clean room' in 1966.

more readily adaptable to passenger car use, these heads were also developed for racing. Gurney used a 305-cid Ford engine with the Mark IV heads in his winning Eagle at Riverside in 1967. By 1968 AAR was making these heads at its own facilities in England and was hoping to get Ford or Lincoln-Mercury interested in selling them, but ironically, the successes the heads enjoyed in racing "only served to strengthen Ford's refusal to be really and truly interested in the things," said Dan in a *Motor Trend* interview. "The fact that they were used twice winning Le Mans in the twenty-four-hour race in 1968 and '69 only further disturbed the people."[3] They were a 'better idea' but not, unfortunately, one that Ford had thought of.

This Gurney Weslake/Eagle engine played an important role in the battle of the engines that raged at Indianapolis in 1968. Strengthened by the addition of Briton Tony Southgate, the AAR staff came up with a

A pair of Mark IV Gurney Weslake heads.

[3] *Motor Trend*, vol 22 (January, 1970), p 93.

stem-to-stern revision of the USAC Eagle layout. The front-end structure was simplified and the nose lowered by moving the springs and shock absorbers outboard and fitting simple two-tube upper wishbones. The monocoque was subtly lower and broader, and the bulkhead at the rear of the engine was made U-shaped so that complete engine/transaxle assemblies could easily be installed and removed.

A flatter rendering of the beak motif was preserved at the nose, and the windscreen was faired back into a raised section extending to the new 1968 Eagle's chopped-off tail. These rear panels were cut and shut in

The new, simpler Eagle right front suspension—Indy, 1968.

Cockpit of Jerry Grant's new 1968 Indy Eagle. Label on the dashboard reads, "This is a race car not a taxi cab."

Gurney (48) passes the Gerhardt-Offy of Bud Tingelstad. Dan took second place in the 1968 Indy 500.

Left: the turbocharged Offy engine in Roger McCluskey's Eagle. Middle: the turbocharged Ford V-8 in Jerry Grant's Eagle. Right: the pushrod power unit in Gurney's second-place car. All were new Eagles at Indy in 1968.

different ways to suit the various engines that were bolted into the five new cars that were made. Roger McCluskey's had a four-cam unblown Ford when it was built, but that engine was changed to one of the new turbocharged Offy engines for the 500, in which it retired. Jerry Grant's car had the troublesome new turbocharged Ford V-8, and also retired. At 1,450 pounds, it was the heaviest of the remarkably light new Eagles.

The three other new cars did rather better. Denny Hulme had an AAR works drive and placed fourth, with an unblown Ford V-8. Second place was seized by Dan Gurney, who after agonizing appraisal had decided to drive the car with the Gurney Eagle Ford engine, Mark IV heads and all. It was producing a peak of 543 bhp at 7800 rpm on a fuel blend containing fifteen percent nitro, and in the new Eagle it performed magnificently. Dan was the only other competitor to finish on the same lap as the Indy winner: Bobby Unser in another 1968 Eagle, lightest of the new brood at 1,370 pounds with its turbo-supercharged Drake Offenhauser engine. Privately owned, Unser's 625-horsepower car had been beautifully prepared by Jud Phillips and was one of the first cars to lap Indy at better than 170 mph.

This at last was the kind of success that Gurney and Goodyear had hoped for when the AAR venture was launched. Dan had proved a point, taking second place with his own modified Ford engine, and Unser's vic-

Denny Hulme was fourth at Indy in 1968 with an Eagle-Ford.

27

Bobby Unser won the 1968 Indy 500 in this Eagle-Offy owned by Leader Card Racers.

tory in a non-AAR car was excellent and obvious validation of the quality of the Eagles that AAR built for sale. And there were more good things in store for Eagles in 1968. With his own Gurney Eagle power, Dan won USAC road races at Mosport and Riverside. Bobby Unser won USAC 150-mile races at Las Vegas, Trenton and Phoenix. These points, added to those he gained at Indy, earned him the USAC National Driving Championship for 1968.

If Dame Fortune was smiling at last on the hard-working AAR crew in Santa Ana, it was perhaps because her scowl toward the Grand Prix racing branch of the team had never been blacker. In 1967 it had seemed that good times were ahead for the Formula 1 Eagle abroad, but in 1968 ... well ... that story deserves a chapter of its own.

Barely leading Mark Donohue's Eagle,
Dan is on his way to his second (1968)
Rex Mays 300 victory at Riverside.

2 Grand Prix Eagle

Though a Grand Prix campaign by AAR was of secondary importance to its major backer, Goodyear, it was of compelling interest to AAR's president and number one driver. Dan Gurney admits that he has always loved road racing first and best. Like all road racers, his personal goal had been the Grand Prix World Driving Championship. In 1961 he showed that this pearl was within his grasp by tying for third in the championship point standings with Stirling Moss. Now that AAR had come into being, however, Gurney had an even more elevated goal: to win that coveted championship in an American Formula 1 car — an Eagle. But ambitious aims often lead to deep frustrations, and so it would be in the three-year history of the Grand Prix Eagle.

Of course Dan Gurney had Grand Prix racing in mind from the first stirrings of the AAR notion. Fate, in the form of Goodyear, did not allow him to make it his main objective, so he and Carroll Shelby had to find ways to build and race Grand Prix cars on the side, ways to finance a Formula 1 campaign as an extension of the USAC effort. Dan was naturally the number one driver, and Jerry Grant was hired by AAR to expedite the building of the cars with a strong incentive: When a second car was ready he was to be its driver.

Though the 1966 Eagle was tailored mainly for Indy use by Gurney and Terry, they managed to compromise its chassis design toward the demands of road racing. This applied to the smaller fuel capacity and also to the roll center heights, which were set low though Terry felt a higher roll axis would have suited Indy better. The use of symmetrical suspension for the USAC Eagle helped generate track-testing data of value to the Grand Prix version while easing the spare-parts problem. The four G.P. monocoques that were completed early in 1966 had thinner skins than the Indy models, of 18 swg aluminum, a change that accounted for the lion's share of the fifty pounds by which the G.P. chassis was lightened.

Other chassis features were carried over intact from the Indy model. The rearmost ring bulkhead was made in two parts instead of one to ease assembly. Intended at first only for the Indy cars, the automatic-feeding oil tank in the cockpit was used on the G.P. models too, to satisfy an unexpected thirst for oil. Considered but not tried, under the pressure of time, was the fitting of a second brake disc and caliper on the inboard end of each of the live front-wheel spindles to increase the braking power at the front. Gordon Schroeder's rack-and-pinion steering was retained, and a five-speed Hewland transaxle, the DG300 model, was used. Gurney encouraged the production of this very useful transmission.

Maintenance of the G.P. Eagles took place in Rye on the south coast of England, where AAR had established a shop to be closer to the Grand Prix action. It was also right next door to Weslake and Co. Ltd., who were to build special three-liter, twelve-cylinder engines for the Formula 1 Eagles. The link between Gurney and Weslake was Frank Aubrey Woods. With B.R.M. since 1946, first as a draftsman and later as chief engine designer, Woods became well acquainted with Gurney when Dan drove the Bourne cars in 1960.

In 1963 the Owen Organisation, backers of the B.R.M., bought the shares of the engine development company founded by Harry Weslake, a veteran of motorcycle engine preparation who had demonstrated a knack for extracting more power from both production and racing auto engines. Woods was transferred from B.R.M. to Weslake where, as chief designer, he worked on new B.R.M. engine design proposals for the three-liter Grand Prix Formula that took effect in 1966. The Weslake-Woods suggestion for a V-12 engine with four valves per cylinder was turned down by B.R.M. but was judged worthy, within Weslake, of testing in the form of a 500 cc twin. By the summer of 1965 this was giving results good

Aubrey Woods, creator of the mechanical design of the Weslake V-12 engine.

(*Overleaf*) Press release photo of the Grand Prix Eagle-Climax (less mirrors, inlet and exhaust systems). The first Eagle to be shown to the public, April 1966. Knock-off hubs were later given up to save weight.

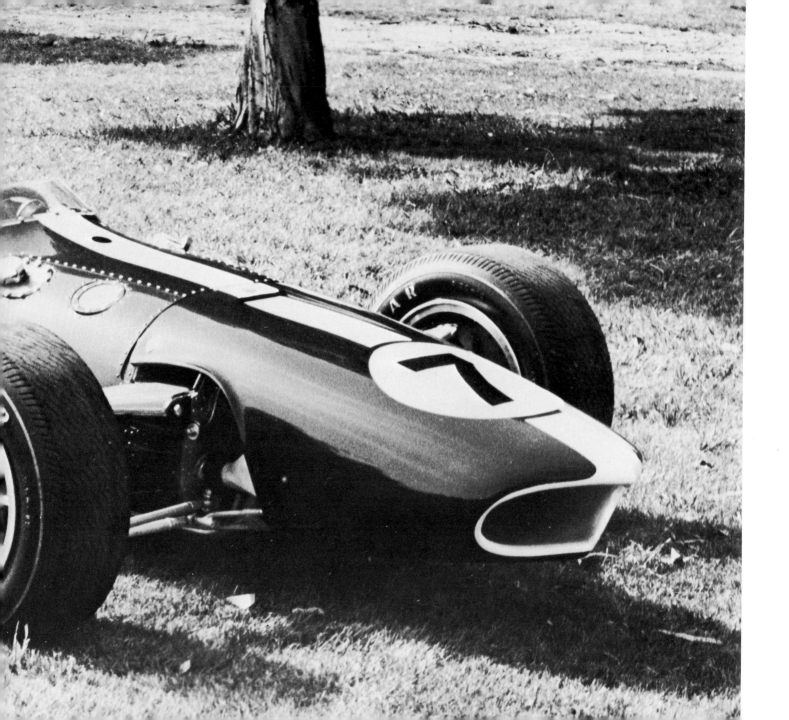

enough to warrant a contact with Dan Gurney to see whether he'd be interested in a twelve for his new Eagle.

There were several reasons why a tie with Weslake might have been considered risky. One was that Weslake was still principally owned by Owen, whose B.R.M. would be an Eagle competitor. Another was that the little Weslake firm had never built a complete automobile engine of any kind, let alone one for a Grand Prix car. But Weslake was dead keen to go motor racing; Gurney liked his engine concept very much, and the price was right. In August, Woods started work on the final design, and in October, 1965, AAR contracted with Weslake for six engines and for space at Rye, Sussex, to build a shop where the G.P. Eagles would be headquartered and maintained. This branch of AAR was named Anglo American Racers in recognition of its divided origins.

At the British AAR base Gurney gathered another cadre of quiet, competent men. Team manager was Bill Dunne, with a background in photography and race officiating. Chief mechanic was Tim Wall, who had been with Brabham for the six years that included Dan's three with that Grand Prix team. Others on the staff were Jo Ramirez and Rouem 'Haff' Haffenden, who specialized in chassis work; Mike Lowman, who handled any necessary metal bending; and apprentice Jesse Corke. A healthy sense of humor flourished within this close-knit group, as it does in many racing teams, but not with the wicked practical joking that was the hallmark of the head office in Santa Ana.

As the first months of 1966 flew by it became increasingly clear to Dan Gurney that the new Grand Prix season would not wait for the completion of the Weslake-built V-12 engine. As a stopgap, AAR was forced to buy some 2.7-liter, four-cylinder Coventry-Climax engines, slightly enlarged versions of the British-made 2.5-liter Climaxes that had been used in G.P. racing through 1960. Two were bought from Webster Racing Enterprises in California, and one each from Racing Preparation Ltd. and the Parnell Team in Britain. The best one (their outputs ranged from 190 to 235 bhp) was put into the first chassis, AAR-101, and taken to Goodwood for its maiden outing on May 8. There the main impression

Dan in his Grand Prix Eagle during the 1966 season.

was of violent vibration from the big four. This was reduced, but not eliminated, by bedding the engine in rubber.

Differences of opinion over starting money kept the Eagle-Climax from making its first race appearance at Monaco, so its maiden race was the exceedingly fast and thus much less suitable Belgian Grand Prix at Spa. Nursing an engine that had failed a piston in practice, Gurney's Eagle was the seventh car to finish, after being last on the grid, but didn't cover enough distance to be classified. Remarkably, Dan did even better at the even faster Reims circuit on July 3. There he placed fifth in the French Grand Prix, collecting the first two World Championship points to be awarded an Eagle driver.

Fine tuning of the Grand Prix Eagle chassis took place during these early-season races. A need for more steering lock at the front wheels was satisfied by putting kinks in the back legs of the lower wishbones. Mercedes-Benz steering dampers were installed at each steering arm to suppress some kickback from the road to the wheel. Then Dan tried eliminating the front anti-dive geometry, the same change he made successfully in the Indy Eagles.

All these improvements came together for the first time in the British Grand Prix, held at Brands Hatch on July 16. There Dan's first practice lap brought out his famous sunny smile. The Eagle's handling, already good, was now excellent. On improved Goodyear tires, the Eagle was suddenly as close to the front of the grid — third fastest — as it had been near the rear in its first two appearances. It held second place in the race until broken piston ring lands forced retirement. Engine troubles also grounded the flying Eagle at the subsequent Dutch Grand Prix, where Dan both qualified and ran fourth in the field.

By this time, in late July, 1966, the Weslake V-12 was long overdue for an appearance in the Eagle. So John Miller at Santa Ana rebuilt and further developed the 2.7-liter Climax, bringing its power level to 255 bhp with new pistons forged in the U.S. Various problems in practice for the August 7 German Grand Prix kept Dan from qualifying well with the revived Climax. From the third row of the grid he moved up to fourth place, of which he was robbed on the last lap by a broken condenser bracket that dropped him to seventh at the finish.

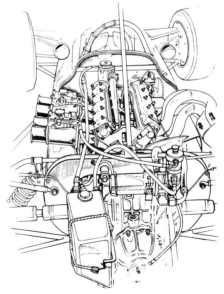

The four-cylinder dohc Climax engine of Eagle AAR-101.

Two pit views of the 1966 G.P. season—
Left: Spa, Belgium, the first race for the
Eagle, where it placed seventh. Right:
Monza, Italy, which was the first outing
of the Weslake V-12; chassis 102. The
man with the cowboy hat is team
manager Bill Dunne.

For the Italian Grand Prix on September 4, 1966, Gurney again qualified with the Climax engine, but the car he brought to his grid position was powered — for the first time — by the Weslake V-12. Visitors to the AAR pits at Monza were astonished by the engine's small size and apparent simplicity. Though they didn't know it at the time, they were being given a glimpse of the future; this was the first racing engine to embody top-end design features that would be commonplace a decade later. The engine had four valves per cylinder at a narrow included angle (thirty degrees) that allowed a single cover to enclose both the close-spaced camshafts on each bank. This would later be thought of as a Cosworth design trademark, but it first appeared on the track in this Weslake Type 58 engine for AAR.

Of the classical sixty-degree-vee layout, this twelve had a larger bore than stroke (72.8 × 60 mm) but the differential was not so extreme as was then widely recommended. Harry Weslake's aim, validated by the 500-cc test engine results, was to maintain good power and torque over a wide speed range with a compact combustion chamber and judiciously-sized ports, not too small to be restrictive but small enough to keep gas speeds up to maintain an inertial ram effect. Similar dimensions (73.3 × 59.2 mm) had also worked well in the two-liter B.R.M. V-8 engine with which Aubrey Woods was entirely familiar.

In the details of its mechanical design the V-12 was reminiscent of the techniques used successfully at B.R.M. on the 1.5-liter V-8 and the two-liter unit developed from it. The crankcase was the same, with seven instead of five main bearings, its ribbed sides extending down well past the crank centerline and embracing close-fitting two-bolt bearing caps. As in the B.R.M., only the rear main cap was cross-bolted. Also identical to the B.R.M. was the cylinder design, with thin-wall cast-iron wet liners held in place by a top flange nipped between the cylinder head and the closed top face of the block. The connecting rods were the same length and design as those used by B.R.M., and the piston mechanical design below the crown was also the same, with narrow slipper skirts and only two rings.

At the top end the valve gear details — apart from the use of four valves per cylinder — were pure B.R.M. in all these respects: dual coil springs, cup-type tappets placed above the springs, a bolted-in ferrous carrier for each tappet, and camshaft support by crowded-roller bearings, each in a steel carrier that also formed the outer race, held down by two capscrews. A departure from Bourne methods was Woods' design of the cylinder head casting to suit both banks of the vee. It made manufacturing and servicing easier.

Valve sizes were 1.2 and 0.985 inches for the inlets and exhausts respectively; and, in the same order, the valve lifts were 0.375 and 0.312 inches. Short stub manifolds down the center of the vee joined each cylinder's separate inlet ports together to a single throat that was fed fuel by a Lucas injector nozzle. The camshafts were driven by a train of gears carried by a separate split magnesium casing at the front of the engine. The block and heads were cast of aluminum alloy, holding the engine's weight to 390 pounds.

Gears below the crankshaft nose drove the water pump, with its twin outlets, and the pressure and scavenge oil pumps. From the timing gears other accessories were turned: the alternator and the two Lucas ignition distributors. Woods had originally planned to put more accessories at the front but he moved them rearward instead to keep the twelve short enough to fit into the space in the Eagle chassis that Len Terry had allotted to the Indy Ford V-8. Driven from the rear ends of the camshafts were the mechanical fuel pump (left exhaust), the Lucas ignition trigger (right exhaust), and the fuel injection distributor/controller (by cogged belt from the right inlet camshaft).

Under the direction of Harry Weslake's stepson, Michael Daniel, equipment was installed at Rye so that the major elements of the twelve could be machined there. A special shed for engine testing was built and equipped with two dynamometers coupled together to give the required torque capacity. During August, 1966, the first engine was assembled, a job requiring 1,200 man-hours; and by the eighteenth it was deemed ready for dyno testing. First it was motored cold with a small diesel donkey engine, and then was fired up and carefully run in.

After a week on the test bed the first V-12 was yielding over one hundred horsepower more than the Climax: 364 bhp at 9500 rpm. "We were now sufficiently confident," said Aubrey Woods, "to want to see just what the engine could do in a car. The Italian Grand Prix at Monza was only one week away, so it was decided to take the car and engine to do a two-fold job: (1) to show the flag and (2) to see what problems would be raised under actual installation and race conditions."

It would have been better, as others at AAR had argued, to test the twelve in private first. It had not propelled the car before its arrival at Monza, where its installation in chassis AAR-102 was completed in the paddock during Friday practice. Dan was unable to make a full practice lap under power because the fuel system caused the engine to cut out under acceleration out of corners. While the mechanics struggled with the too-new twelve, Dan and Phil Hill practiced in the Eagle-Climax. Though Dan's best lap in the V-12 was twenty seconds off the pace, he elected to drive it in the race to give it the seasoning that only actual competition can provide. (Hill wasn't fast enough in the Eagle four to qualify.) The fuel feed troubles were further aggravated by full tanks, and with a rising oil temperature, Gurney gave up after seventeen of the sixty-eight laps.

Both cars went to North America for the last two races of the '66 season at Watkins Glen, New York and Mexico City. In its post-Monza teardown the V-12 had shown no mechanical faults, and no special clues to the causes of various thromboses in its cooling and lubricating systems. Now on the Glen course the engine pumped oil from every crevice and shot its oil and water temperature needles off their dials. Under these conditions Dan completed only fifteen laps, from an indifferent grid position, before retiring.

In Mexico the twelve was given to Bob Bondurant, who had driven the Eagle-Climax at the Glen and who had been disqualified for receiving outside assistance after leaving the track to avoid a wreck. In Mexico City Dan eked out a fifth-place finish with a lame Climax engine while Bondurant had to retire the Eagle-Weslake with fuel feed faults even though he'd been holding the revs down to 8500 rpm to minimize the oil pumping problem. Gurney raced the Climax-powered AAR-101 one more time,

The Weslake V-12 was still troublesome at the Watkins Glen U.S. Grand Prix. Here the engine's plugs are being changed.

Left: Dan in the Eagle-Weslake. Right: Bob Bondurant in the Eagle-Climax. Both at the 1966 U.S. Grand Prix.

Dan with the four-cylinder Coventry Climax at the Mexico Grand Prix in 1966.

retiring with chassis trouble in South Africa on January 2, 1967, before selling it to a sponsor, Castrol, for Canadian Al Pease to drive.

Castrol's backing of AAR in 1967 supplanted that of Mobil, which had decided not to get further involved with racing after the '66 season. This still left the AAR Grand Prix effort drastically underfinanced. "We are a small outfit," said Gurney early in 1967, "with meager backing, and spread pretty thin at this point. Any kind of setback will be felt keenly. For instance, if we lose an engine, one car probably won't race." Engine loss seemed less likely, because the oil blowby problem had been tracked to excessive clearances in the cylinder liner fits and, they hoped, had been rectified.

The AAR European season opened with a brilliant victory in a Grand Prix, but unfortunately not one that counted for championship points. Dan and his new teammate, fellow Californian Richie Ginther, dominated the two heats of the Race of Champions at Brands Hatch on March 12, and Gurney won the final. He had a new 413-bhp engine in chassis AAR-102, with which he'd managed to do some pre-Brands testing at record knots at Goodwood. Richie's car, which was completed the Wednesday before the race, was a new chassis AAR-103 carrying the original V-12, said to be delivering 409 bhp. They were running one-two in the final until trouble with experimental brake pads forced Ginther to retire.

The power certainly seemed to be there. Said Dan, "It was very exciting to see that both Richie and I were able to out-accelerate anything on the starting grid, including the Honda, which has been regarded as the 'dragster' of the Grand Prix cars." Nor was it a hollow victory. Ferraris and Brabhams were among those outpaced by Dan's Eagle. Gurney had beaten the best of the best at Brands Hatch while recording the first Grand Prix victory by an American driver in an American car since Jimmy Murphy's celebrated win in the 1921 French Grand Prix with a Duesenberg.

This was encouraging, but Gurney and Ginther knew the coming Lotus-Cosworth would be tough competition, especially in the area where they were far off the pace: light weight. Though the minimum weight per-

The mag-ti lightweight Eagle AAR-104 at Santa Ana in May, 1967, shown with provisional body parts just after completion.

missible under the F.I.A. Formula 1 rules was 500 kilograms, (1,100 pounds), the dry weight of the Eagle-Weslake was 1,280 pounds. It was carrying a weight penalty equal to the heft of an invisible passenger. His search for a solution he could afford led Dan Gurney to California's Harvey Aluminum, the company that had sponsored the Buick-powered Mickey Thompson car in which Dan first raced at Indy in 1962. Harvey became an important backer of AAR in 1967.

Harvey's recommendations included the use of magnesium instead of aluminum in the monocoque frame, and the replacement of steel suspension parts with titanium, which offers comparable strength at less weight. Early in April the AAR fabricators, notably shop chief Pete Wilkins and welder Dick Weber, started working experimentally with these new materials. Harvey gave them a 'purge box' for welding titanium, a sealed enclosure from which air must be evacuated before titanium can be successfully welded inside it. At the end of the third week of April, when they'd gained some confidence in their ability to tame magnesium and titanium, they were assigned the job of employing these metals in the building of a complete new Grand Prix Eagle chassis. And they were given a target: to have it ready for the Dutch Grand Prix on June 4, 1967.

For Richie Ginther, who had taken over from Jerry Grant the role of Dan's alter ego — to expedite such AAR programs as the new light chassis — the weeks ahead were bittersweet. He missed qualifying for one of the sixteen starting places at Monaco by a half-second margin. (AAR was not, remarkably, yet recognized as an 'official works team.') In that race on May 7, Dan climbed through the field from eighth at the start to a strong third place, which he lost on the fourth lap when the cogged belt to the Lucas fuel metering unit broke. Then the AAR focus was switched to Indianapolis, where Ginther stepped out of his Eagle ride, feeling he was no longer able to race at competitive speeds.

His absence from Indiana allowed Richie to be at Goodwood in the last week of May to test the first mag-ti Eagle, so nicknamed for its novel materials. Bearing serial number AAR-104, it differed visibly from the earlier frames in the very fine and close riveting of the hot-formed magnesium skin to the steel formers. All the wishbones and links at front and rear were made of titanium, and typical of the weight-saving thereby was the reduction of the upper front wishbone from 3⅜ pounds in mild steel to slightly below two pounds in titanium. A big challenge successfully surmounted was the crafting of the exhaust headers in titanium, reducing their weight to 16½ pounds from the 36½ pounds the steel headers scaled. In all, eighty-eight pounds were peeled off, cutting the poundage of the mag-ti Eagle to 1,192. Later a new aluminum chassis, AAR-103, was given the new titanium running gear to trim its weight, and some aluminum castings on the Weslake engine were changed to magnesium.

With the new car Gurney was convincingly fast at Zandvoort, Holland, being nipped for fastest qualifying time at the last moment by Graham Hill in the brand-new Lotus-Cosworth which, said Dan, "showed immediately that it will be as tough as we thought. Our fuel metering unit gave us trouble from the start, and in a very few laps our engine died." Another car had been entered for Ginther, who had, however, elected not to drive.

Left: Nose of the aluminum chassis Eagle (AAR-103) with titanium suspension pieces at the 1967 Canadian G.P. Right: The lighter mag-ti car (AAR-104) at the U.S. Grand Prix in 1967.

La Source hairpin at Spa-Francor-
champs, 1967: *this was the day!*

Only one Eagle, AAR-104, was entered for the Belgian Grand Prix at Spa. It proved to be the right Eagle. Dan put it in the middle of the front row of the grid, from which he raced among the leaders on this most demanding of the Grand Prix circuits. Chasing Jackie Stewart's sixteen-cylinder B.R.M. Dan set a new lap record for Spa at 148.85 mph, on lap nineteen. When the B.R.M. had passed the Eagle early in the race, Dan had seen an oil leak that he was sure would bring the British car to its heels sooner or later. 'Sooner' came on the twenty-first of twenty-eight laps, when Stewart slowed, struggling with an oil-less gearbox, and Gurney passed him in full view of the crowd near the pits. Dan held the lead to the finish to score the first triumph for an Eagle in a World Championship Grand Prix. It is also, at this writing, the last such triumph.

"My fuel pressure was running so low during the race," said Gurney afterward, "that I thought I wasn't going to make it at first and in fact made a hasty pit stop to tell our mechanics what was wrong. But I went right back out, and went on to win by 63 seconds. Spa was no fluke. We were running as fast as Lotus on the straights, if not faster." It was a day of tremendous personal fulfillment for Daniel Gurney. Reported *The New York Times*, June 19, 1967: "A week ago, Gurney and A.J. Foyt of Houston won the 24 Hours of Le Mans in a Ford Mark IV. On the victory stand, Gurney sprayed champagne over everyone in sight. Here, with no champagne on the victory stand, he plucked flowers from a huge wreath and threw them to the crowd. Obviously, here is a man who knows how to win."

AAR came to the next race, the French Grand Prix on the Bugatti Circuit at Le Mans, with its strength redoubled. Bruce McLaren joined the team and put AAR-102 on the second row of the grid, while Dan had his now-usual front-row position in AAR-104. Both retired, Gurney while vying for the lead, with engine troubles that seemed to be trivial: breakages of pipes and accessory drives. At the British G.P. on July 15, however, engine failures became grave and epidemic. Neither car finished, and the weekend's tally was three broken V-12's, two of them with broken connecting rods and all the damage usually attendant thereto.

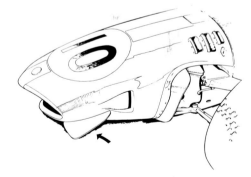

Late in the 1967 season the Eagle G.P. car had spoilers aside the air inlet and spoilers on the outlets for warm air from the back of the water/oil radiator, to improve cooling.

The Gurney-McLaren duo appeared once more, in the German Grand Prix, a race Dan Gurney should have won. With three of the fifteen laps to go and a lead of three-quarters of a minute in hand, and a new lap record in his pocket, his Eagle broke a universal-joint cross on one of the rear half-shafts. McLaren was out with engine failure on lap four. Gurney received small solace from his third-place finish in the next Grand Prix at Mosport, Canada, in the same chassis he drove at Monaco, AAR-103, here with titanium running gear. And the Italian Grand Prix at Monza, a race in which the powerful Eagle-Weslake should have starred, was a disaster. One engine failed in practice and two came unglued in the race, in Gurney's car (104) while leading and in Ludovico Scarfiotti's Eagle (103). After only six of the sixty-eight laps both blue-and-white cars were silent in the pits.

AAR-104 went to America as a lone entry for Dan, with an engine patched together from the best remaining bits, and retired at the Glen (suspension breakage) and at Mexico City (starting-line damage to the

The 1967 Canadian G.P.: Al Pease in AAR-101; the Eagle-Climax now in private hands.

radiator). There was not even a lap record (as at the German G.P.) to show that the Eagle had been there. "We're trying to do things on a shoestring," Dan admitted at the time. "We've had to be satisfied with a relatively small amount of testing. Testing is what knocks out unreliability. We haven't wanted to do the testing in the races themselves, but that's what it keeps boiling down to. Many times what looks like an economy move turns out to be more expensive in the long run."

Sharp changes were clearly needed at the end of a season that, after such a promising start, saw Dan Gurney only eighth in the World Driving Championship standings. The engines were a manifest point of weakness. Their reliability level was so erratic and unpredictable that AAR could only conclude that the tolerances to which they were being made and assembled by Weslake weren't precise enough. Negotiations in October led to a new monthly-basis agreement with Weslake, taking effect in November, under which AAR would assemble the engines from parts made by Weslake. AAR hired Doug Orchard to supervise this work.

As is almost always the case when responsibility is divided, this system was an utter failure. Its first and only test was the South African Grand Prix on January 1, 1968. There Dan could reach no higher than the midpoint of the grid and was forced to retire from the race with overheating and terminal oil leakage. This was bad enough; what followed was even worse. A spare engine was installed to test some tires for Goodyear at Kyalami, after the G.P., and turned out to be in poorer shape than the one that had caused Gurney to pull out of the race!

Dan had given Weslake every possible chance to make good. He knew the design had promise, and he knew the Weslake crew had done its best with a limited budget and outmoded machine tools. "Weslake's did a good job up to a point," Dan said later, "but that wasn't enough." Acting out of necessity, without the bitterness to which he might have been entitled, Gurney severed AAR's links with Weslake and set up his own plant in England for building and testing engines.

Understandably, it took some time to put the new operation in place. Not until April 1 did the office staff move to new premises in a 4,500-square-foot building at Ashford, about fifteen miles northeast of

Tim Wall (left), Dan and Jo Ramirez in the paddock at the 1967 Canadian G.P. with Eagle AAR-103.

The Weslake V-12, at the 1967 U.S. Grand Prix, then said to be producing 416 bhp at 10,250 rpm.

Rye, where they were joined by a new AAR employee, Aubrey Woods. On April 15 the chassis work was moved there, and by May 1, with the establishment of the engine shop, Anglo American Racers was based entirely at Ashford.

Before the '68 season began, Gurney had hoped for fifty horsepower more from better-built Weslake engines. (The original projection of the twelve's potential had been 480 bhp.) His first rude shock was that he had less power than he thought, not more. Tony Rudd of B.R.M. offered Dan the use of the test bed at Bourne, remarking, with his usual dry humor, that it should be easy to install the Weslake engine there since its crankcase was the same as that of B.R.M.'s own V-12. On the B.R.M. dynamometer, which was not known as one of the most pessimistic in Britain, the Gurney-Weslake developed no more than 390 horsepower.

The Spanish Grand Prix in May was given a bye while the new Eagle Mark 1A engine, as it was designated, was made ready. At Monaco Dan was relegated to the very back of the grid; this time he was saved from displacement by faster independents because of AAR's recognition as an 'official works team.' Absences of sparks and oil pressure held him to only ten laps in the race.

"The Belgian, Dutch and French G.P.'s were passed up," wrote Max Muhleman to members of the AAR Eagle Club, "as engineer Doug Orchard, designer Aubrey Woods and their staff labored mightily to again overhaul the competition. The first of the new mills was rushed into an appearance at the British G.P. Improved performance was obvious, but it was too soon and Dan retired in hopes of having all well next time out. The German race had hopes soaring when Gurney surged to third on a dark, wet day, but a cut tire sustained some seven miles out on the Nürburgring course consumed a crippling amount of time and left Gurney 16th and last by the time he finally returned. The Eagle flew swiftly the remainder of the race, however, with laps faster than the leaders' bringing Dan back to ninth at the flag." It was the only Grand Prix Eagle finish of the year.

"At Italy came the big decision," continued Muhleman. "Race weekend was hot, dry and, as always at Monza, fast. In brief, the Eagle

V-12 was not ready to flex its muscles and muscle was the only answer for the Autodrome. Driving hard, Gurney picked his way from 13th to 7th but temperatures were up dangerously and at last oil pressure dropped under the impossible strain. Out again. And worse, not competitive." For AAR, which took special pride in its ability to generate pure speed, this last was the cruelest cut of all.

During Monza practice Dan had tried the spare car of another Goodyear-backed team, McLaren. By the day after the race he had ar-

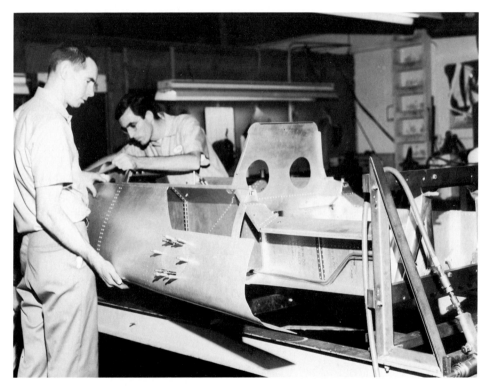

Plant superintendent, Pete Wilkins (left) and Terry Malone, fitter, work on the all-magnesium monocoque Eagle that was to have been raced in 1969.

ranged to drive that car, under Olsonite sponsorship, in the last three G.P.s of the season. This was only a temporary measure, AAR assured its supporters: "We will be back next year with a new Eagle and a fully-developed V-12." During the fall of 1968 the monocoque frame of this new Eagle was being completed at Santa Ana. Its designer was Tony Southgate, who had been with AAR since late 1967. Its skin was magnesium inside and out. It was a narrower, slimmer, flat-bottomed car, with outboard mounting of the front suspension, planned to be right down to the 1,100-pound limit. Thought was also being given to building a similar car to accept the Cosworth-Ford V-8 engine.

In November, under the chill glare of reality, these plans were abandoned. Said Dan to *Autoweek*, "We're the only outfit that has been actively competing in Indianapolis, Can-Am, and Grand Prix racing. It is very apparent that we're just spread too thin. We're not big enough to do it. Therefore we were faced with a decision."[4] That decision was to give up Grand Prix competition. In spite of his virtual eclipse in 1968 Dan was asked to lead two Grand Prix teams in 1969, but he rejected these offers to give his full attention to racing on the American side of the Atlantic.

The Ashford plant was sold, and its personnel dispersed. Dan helped Bill Dunne find a post with STP in Europe, and Aubrey Woods went back to B.R.M. A buyer was sought for the V-12 engine (Honda expressed some interest) in vain. The 1969 Grand Prix season opened without an Eagle entry and was all the poorer for that. An era of American Grand Prix participation had come to a close. But Dan Gurney and AAR had not stopped thinking of ways to set the stars and stripes flying again from the Formula 1 flagpoles.

[4] *Autoweek*, vol 18 (December 7, 1968), p 5.

Continental and Can-Am

Late in the 1960's, Eagles and Eagle-ized cars were active in American road racing: in the Can-Am series from 1966 through 1969 and in the Continental Championship in 1968 and 1969. AAR fielded works entries in the internationally-recognized Can-Am, and had only a solitary victory by Dan to show for its efforts. For the Continental, AAR only built cars, entering none of its own, and had the pleasure of seeing its private owners collect the Championship in the only two seasons in which competitive Formula A Eagles were on the market. Such are the vicissitudes of motor racing that it would probably be unwise to draw any conclusions from these contrasting histories. Their net effect, combined with the team's USAC activities, was that it was hard to escape seeing Eagles and dark blue AAR entries on all America's major race tracks in 1968 and '69.

While AAR used modified cars from other makers in the Can-Am series, the machines it built for the Continental were pure American Eagle. Their creation was inspired by the program for single-seat, open-wheel formula-car racing that was developed by the Sports Car Club of America in 1967 and expanded in 1968. In the first of those years, classes were established for three engine sizes. The largest, called Formula A, admitted unblown racing engines of up to three liters — the international Grand Prix limit. The breakthrough that attracted AAR and others came in 1968, when engines of up to five liters based on volume-produced blocks and heads were also admitted to Formula A. Coupled with a simultaneous increase in the number of races from five to nine and a sweeten-

That beautiful Eagle wheel and a Formula A nosepiece; photographed at Lime Rock.

The suspension of the 1968 Formula A Eagle resembled that of the same year's Indianapolis car.

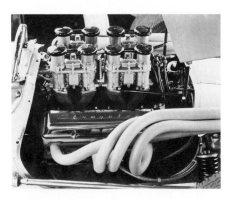

The Weber-carbureted Chevy engine in George Wintersteen's 1968 Formula A Eagle.

ing of the prize kitty from $25,000 to $91,000, this expansion of Formula A drew respectable fields of cars to what the SCCA then called its Grand Prix Championship.

Seizing the opportunity offered by this change in Formula A, Dan Gurney decided to build a suitable variant of the new 1968 Indy Eagle and offer it for sale. Designer Tony Southgate made few changes. The new all-outboard front suspension was fine for road courses as well as ovals, and wheelbase remained at the mandatory Indy minimum of ninety-six inches. The aluminum and steel monocoque was similar to that of the Indy Eagle in design and shape, but was slimmed along its flanks to reduce the fuel tank size to the maximum permissible thirty U.S. gallons. Fiberglass was used for the Eagle-beak nosepiece and the rear bodywork.

AAR charged $11,500 for the Formula A Eagle chassis. This included the brakes, which were Girling discs at first and later California-made Airhearts, with 11.75-inch ventilated discs, but did not include wheels, engine or transaxle. Buyers normally chose the Eagle magnesium wheels, of fifteen-inch diameter and eleven- and sixteen-inch width at front and rear respectively. Shock absorbers were adjustable Konis, and the rack-and-pinion steering gear demanded only 1.1 turns from lock to lock.

The 1968 chassis was conformed to suit the five-liter Chevrolet V-8 engine, basically the unit used in the Camaro Z-28. Equipped with Weber carburetors and modified by such specialists as Traco, this well-seasoned engine developed more than 400 horsepower at reliable speeds of 7000 rpm and above. Drive was usually through a triple-disc eight-inch clutch to a Hewland LG600 transaxle with five forward speeds. So equipped, a Formula A Eagle with oil and water aboard typically weighed 1,470 pounds, distributed sixty percent to the rear (with the driver in place).

Two of these cars were active in the '68 series, their main opposition being the new Lola Type 140 and the American-built McKee. Only once in eight races, however, did anything but an Eagle win. The Grand Prix Championship went to the only driver to run in all eight events, Dr. Lou Sell, who won five of them outright. Backed by Wynn's oil, his Eagle was a frequent visitor to Santa Ana for maintenance. Second in the Championship standings was George Wintersteen's Eagle-Chevy, a

beautifully-prepared car which won two events, at Lime Rock and Donnybrooke.

This dominance attracted more buyers to AAR's offerings for the 1969 series, which was renamed the Continental Championship and further expanded to thirteen races at as many tracks in the U.S. and Canada. The successful '68 Formula A Eagle was changed only in detail. To accommodate engines other than the ubiquitous Chevy, to suit buyers such as the Chrysler-Plymouth dealer who ordered two cars, the monocoque from the cockpit back was, with some difficulty, considerably reshaped.

Wings, which appeared only tentatively in 1968, were Eagle options in 1969. (The Grand Prix Eagle sprouted a low rear wing toward the end of the 1968 season.) The AAR designers created their own airfoil sections empirically and applied them to front stub wings thirteen inches long and to a high rear wing forty-five inches in span, mounted directly atop the rear hub carriers. Adjustable in attack angle for chassis tuning, the new wing array was track-tested by Dan Gurney early in 1969. Later in the season some cars were fitted with new noses, with added vents that allowed air to escape upward from the radiator.

Thompson Raceway, 1968: Left: George Wintersteen's Eagle-Chevy Formula A car placed fourth in this event and was second in the series championship. Right: Dr. Lou Sell's Eagle-Chevy won this race and the series championship.

Another view of Lou Sell's Formula A championship Eagle.

Views of the new 1969 Formula A Eagle monocoque under construction in Santa Ana in October of 1968.

John Cannon was fourth in the 1969 Formula A championship.

Carbureted engines were still normal wear in 1969 though some competitors, such as John Cannon in the Malcolm Starr Eagle-Chevy, successfully pioneered the Lucas injection that was later universally used. His Traco-built Chevy produced 468 bhp at 7500 rpm early in 1969. Cannon won three of the Continental races, boosting him to a fourth-place ranking in the Championship. Number one on that list was Tony Adamowicz, who won only two races but placed consistently in many others in his Eagle-Chevy. Other Eagle-Chevrolet drivers ranking in the top ten in the Continental Championship were Sam Posey (third) and Bob Brown (sixth).

AAR elected not to defend its laurels with a new-design Formula A Eagle in 1970. Though older Eagles continued to compete, they were pushed well down the finishing lists by the more advanced British chassis (Lola, McLaren, Surtees, Lotus) that were being built as Formula A racing — known as Formula 5000 abroad — began to boom in popularity in Europe. Though race placings as high as second and third were recorded, the best-

John Cannon at speed in his Malcolm Starr Eagle-Chevy during the 1969 season.

ranked Eagle in the 1970 Championship was that of Dave Jordan, twelfth. Rex Ramsey and Hiroshi Fushida were fourteenth and eighteenth in the final Continental standings. Thus did Eagles quietly fade from the SCCA's Formula-car series — until 1974 (see Chapter 6).

The fuel-injected Unser-prepared Chevy engine of Bob Brown's Formula A Eagle.

Bob Brown's Eagle-Chevy placed fourth in the 1969 Formula A race at Lime Rock Park, and seventh in the series.

In parallel, AAR was also patronizing, if erratically, the SCCA's premier professional road-racing series. This was the rich Canadian-American Challenge Cup, known the world over as the Can-Am. Recognized by the F.I.A. with international listings, the Can-Am was open to the world's best drivers in sports cars governed by Group 7 regulations. These set the various dimensions of fenders, cockpit, etc. that made the cars 'sports cars,' while enforcing no weight minima or engine size maxima. This was a formula that had a magnetic attraction for the real racers, for men like John Surtees, Chris Amon, Bruce McLaren, Denny Hulme, Jim Hall, Mark Donohue — and Dan Gurney.

All American Racers, which traced its beginnings to sports car racing, kept on supporting that branch of motor sport through 1970. It did so by modifying cars from other makers, not with purebred Eagles, but usually with Gurney Weslake Ford engines. In fact the first such engine to race was the Mark II version in a sports car event, the 1965 Riverside Grand Prix. Installed in Gurney's McLaren at the eleventh hour, it showed great potential. The first victory for this engine also came in a sports car, on May 22, 1966, at Bridgehampton. That was a win by Jerry Grant in the Vanderbilt Cup race (part of the SCCA's U.S. Road Racing Championship series) in an AAR Lola Type 70 powered by a Mark III model Gurney Weslake Ford.

Jerry Grant on his way to winning the 1966 Bridgehampton USRRC in an AAR-entered Type 70 Lola with a Gurney Weslake/Ford engine.

Dan himself took over this dark blue Lola in the fall of 1966 for the first round of Can-Am races. With a 305-cubic inch engine producing 520 bhp at 7800 rpm, he outraced the formidable winged Chaparrals, in their debut event, to win the Can-Am at Bridgehampton. He was fastest qualifier in the next event at Mosport Park and set the fastest lap while taking the lead, which he lost when a crankshaft broke. Dan's story was similar — fast, then breaking — in the last three Can-Ams on the West Coast. But he had garnered a single victory, his only personal win of the 1966 season and the most important one to the credit of AAR that year.

It was another 'wait 'til next year' Can-Am season for AAR in 1967. Wrote Dan to Eagle Club members at the end of that year, "The only bright spot in our Can-Am participation this fall was the pole position we achieved at Riverside ahead of the works McLarens which had so dominated the races and qualifying. It was a short-lived success, but it is in the record book and we can be proud of it. While we were the best-running Ford in the series, it is obvious that we still have some homework to do this winter."

Gurney's Can-Am mount in '67 had again been a Lola, the first of the three lighter Type 70 Mark 3B cars the British firm had produced (chassis no. SL73/122). Connected to its four-speed Hewland LG500 transaxle was an enlarged Gurney Weslake V-8 that used a new high-deck cast-iron Ford block that allowed a bore and stroke of 4 × 3¾ inches for a displacement of 375 cubic inches. This was one of the biggest engines active in the Can-Am that season. It retained the Mark III cylinder heads, which John Miller fitted with Weber carburetors and alternatively, with much less success, Tecalemit-Jackson constant-flow fuel injection. This was an exceedingly potent package but the 1967 Can-Am season ended before it could be rid of nagging flaws.

Planning to convert his engines completely to the new, narrower production-type Mark IV Gurney Weslake heads, Dan sold his Mark III equipment, big blocks and all, to West Coast racer Lothar Motschenbacher at the end of the 1967 season. After experimenting with Robert Bosch fuel injection, Motschenbacher restored the Webers and installed the engines in his new McLaren M6B. Preparing the car himself, Lothar never won but did well enough in 1968 to finish fourth in the final standings of both the USRRC and the Can-Am series.

Unexpectedly, this sale of the 1967 engines jeopardized the chances of AAR's 1968 Can-Am campaign, its most ambitious so far. It found, to its dismay, that Ford was unable to supply more of the special blocks that allowed 375-cid engines to be built. AAR therefore decided to build the lightest and best possible small engines, improve their reliability and construct a light-weight car around them. Placed in charge of this program was a new face at AAR, Phil Remington. One of the authentic geniuses in the art of bending metal to make cars, the 47-year-old Remington had played a pivotal role in the success of the GT40 Mark II Fords under Carroll Shelby and had helped build Lance Reventlow's Scarab sports and Grand Prix cars.

The Olsonite 'McLeagle' during its first appearance at the 1968 Bridgehampton Can-Am. AAR modified an M6B McLaren chassis and inserted a Lucas-injected Gurney Weslake V-8 displacing 325 cubic inches.

As raw material AAR bought a new McLaren M6B, the production replica of the M6A that won the Can-Am Championship in 1968. With the help of Harvey Aluminum, as with the Grand Prix car, the McLaren was lightened by the use of titanium for the suspension wishbones, shift linkage and exhaust headers and was fitted with the distinctive Eagle wheels. This and other work supervised by Remington lightened the McLaren by one hundred pounds and justified its new name: the Olsonite McLeagle. It was powered by a 325-cid Ford engine with Mark IV Gurney Eagle heads, Lucas fuel injection, a special gear drive to the camshaft, and a dry-sump layout similar to that of the Indy Ford engine.

A second string to the AAR team bow in '68 was a new Type 160 Lola with an engine similar to that described above except for its smaller 302-cid displacement. This was driven through most of the Can-Am season by David 'Swede' Savage, a tall, blond Californian just twenty-one years old who was the living proof of Dan Gurney's oft-expressed intention to help young American drivers make headway whenever he had the chance. Impressed by Swede's aplomb and grit on motorcycles and in stock cars, Dan hired him as a member of the AAR team in December, 1967. He drove an AAR Lola in a USRRC race at Riverside in April (placing sixth) and next drove a sports-racer at the Bridgehampton Can-Am in September, finishing fourth. This was two places ahead of his boss, who had stopped at the pits to check the suspension of the McLeagle. The car's steering geometry gave it a tendency to 'hunt' to the left and right over bumps; the effect had been so severe that Dan suspected a leaking tire.

Mechanical troubles kept the Gurney/McLeagle combination from finishing in the next two races, and at Riverside, the penultimate '68 Can-Am, Dan let Swede drive the car with a 325-cid engine. He finished eighth. Dan had taken over the Type 160 Lola and installed a special 427-cid engine that Ford had developed for the Can-Am series, based on Le Mans-type internals encased in aluminum heads and block and fitted with a special cross-ram fuel injection manifold. With this V-8 of 580-plus horsepower, Gurney was at last among the leaders at both Riverside and Las Vegas, the final race, but retired both times.

John Miller with a rare steel-linered aluminum block for the Ford Fairlane V-8 that allowed him to build light, 344-cid engines.

Though Gurney had not been pleased with this big, new Ford engine, when Ford told him it would have an even bigger hemispherical-head 494-cid engine for his use in 1969, he made his plans accordingly. He and his crew were still imbued with the old-school Ford racing spirit. Dan was determined to remain true to the products of the Dearborn company as long as was even remotely possible. But, having built an ambitious '69 Can-Am program around the 494 V-8, which Ford was to supply along with some support money, he was told at the eleventh hour that it wouldn't be available.

This was a body blow to AAR's Can-Am hopes. Gurney went back to Ford and bargained for an alternate engine, an aluminum 396-cid V-8. After many delays this was approved, but by the time the components were delivered to AAR the Can-Am season was to all intents and purposes over. At the last moment the 494-cid engine *did* become available, but not to Gurney, because in the politically-charged atmosphere at Ford somebody had disseminated the canard that he didn't really want the 494, and preferred to run the smaller 396! So unsavory to Dan was all this chicanery that he was particularly receptive when contacted by Plymouth, for whom he signed a contract to race in 1970.

In the meantime there'd been races to run. Since they had to go with a small 344-cid Gurney Eagle engine, the AAR choice was the lightweight McLeagle. Its bodywork was modified, to increase aerodynamic downforce, and it was fitted with high wings above both the front and rear suspensions. This was an ideal formula for the twisty Mosport track on which the Can-Am season opened in June. It allowed Dan to harass Denny Hulme's second-place McLaren until an over-stressed suspension upright on the McLeagle broke at three-fifths distance. It was the engine that broke in practice for the next race at St. Jovite, and since it was the only one they had, Gurney couldn't compete.

AAR sat out the next five Can-Ams while fighting the Ford political wars and trying to develop a dark-horse engine of its own. This was a new Ford-based engine from the fertile brain of John Miller, tracing its origins to 1968. Its special heads had three valves per cylinder in a shallow trefoil-shaped chamber, the doubled-up valves being the inlets, worked

Dan with his protege, Swede Savage, during the 1968 Can-Am season.

Special Mark IV head with modified spark plug positions; were used in the late-1968-season Can-Am engines.

by a forked rocker arm. Unusually, the exhaust ports were in the center of the vee and the inlet ram stacks protruded horizontally at each side. Test-bed running gave exceptional results: 606 bhp at 8500 rpm from 344 cid on gasoline. But when it was tested in a car at Riverside it developed steam pockets in the coolant flow that caused overheating. John Miller: "Just about the time Dan would get warmed up, so would the engine."

So Gurney arrived at Michigan International Speedway for the September 28 Can-Am with an engine in his McLeagle that was sure to exacerbate his friction with Ford: an aluminum 427-cid Chevrolet V-8, an ex-Penske unit, of the type that was powering the all-conquering Team McLaren cars. It wasn't healthy, however, and when Dan was offered a seat in a spare orange McLaren he accepted it. He drove with ease from the back of the grid to third place at the finish. He competed in the next two races with the McLeagle-Chevy, retiring at Laguna Seca and finishing

Left: Swede Savage finished eighth in the 325-cid McLeagle at the 1968 Riverside Can-Am. Right: The exposed McLeagle chassis at Riverside.

fourth at Riverside (wearing only a rear wing), robbed of a higher placing by a leaking head gasket.

As a builder and entrant Dan Gurney found little to enjoy in the 1969 Can-Am season. Yet he hadn't lost his craving to beat the unbeatable McLarens: "We still intend to try and blow the New Zealanders back across the ocean, which will be a formidable task." Instead of beating them, however, he joined them. After Bruce McLaren was killed while testing the new M8D, Dan was offered a drive in this 1970 Can-Am car. In

Gurney's Type 160 Lola with a 427-cid Ford V-8 engine retired with an oil leak after seven laps at the 1968 Riverside Can-Am.

the season-opener at Mosport he had pole position, set the fastest lap, and won the race. In the next race he forfeited only the fastest lap. Gurney had a flying start toward a Can-Am Championship in what would prove to be his last racing season.

In 1970 Dan was also driving Grand Prix cars for the McLaren team, making a return to the G.P. lists after a season and a half away. He had his share of car trouble with the Ford-powered McLaren M14A, which was not a winner that season. Yet Dan enjoyed a great drive at Clermont-Ferrand in France, a real driver's circuit, in July, placing sixth only a whisker from fifth place. Later that month he was lying seventh in the British Grand Prix when he was forced to retire with engine failure. That was Dan's last G.P. race for the McLaren team.

In mid-1970 Gurney had to make one of the toughest decisions of his career. "I was faced with the choice of going with McLaren and losing AAR, really, because it was going to be a full-time job," he said later. The McLaren team needed a driver of Dan's caliber to join Denny Hulme in all its Grand Prix and Can-Am entries in that year and those ahead. But back home AAR's own car-building programs were in trouble, demanding Dan's total attention. His marriage was being dissolved. There were conflicts between Castrol, which had sponsored Gurney and AAR for some years, and Gulf, which was a principal backer of the McLaren team.

Further, Dan didn't feel comfortably at home with the British-based McLaren crew because, he said, "We had been competitors both in the sponsorship arena and on the race track for so many years." This contributed to communication problems between driver and team that Dan knew were not in the best interests of either. He found that "a little difficult, after you've been running your own team." So Dan decided to resign the McLaren ride and, at the end of 1970, to resign from the ranks of active drivers. All American Racers lost a superb driver but gained a dedicated, full-time president.

The '500' Jinx

The three years from 1969 through 1971 were ones of technical turmoil at Indianapolis. They witnessed the rise and perfection of turbocharging, the eclipse of atmospheric induction, radical aerodynamic experiments and the end of four-wheel drive. They also saw the end of the stock-block engine as a viable Indy competitor, in spite of Dan Gurney's second-place finish with one in 1969. That was also Dan's best personal finish in the two years in which he drove (1969 and 1970), and the best placing for an Eagle, during these three years. The gods that held sway over the denizens of Speedway, Indiana during that month of speed in May had determined, it seemed, that Eagle cars would have to be satisfied with that one 500 victory in 1968.

No one can say that Dan Gurney and AAR did not go all-out in search of a triumph at Indianapolis during these vexing years. AAR built fewer cars and lavished more time and effort on each one, making sharp design changes for each season. Nevertheless they were unable to come up with a better blend for a 500-mile victory than the Brabham-inspired Hawk of 1969 and the Lola-inspired Colt of 1970 and 1971 — all powered by turbocharged Fords and, even more galling to AAR's principal backer, all running on Firestone tires.

Though they didn't win at Indy, and in fact never won any race, the model 56 turbine cars that Lotus brought to the Speedway in 1968 profoundly influenced the other competitors by their very fast pace in qualifying, their four-wheel drive, and their bold and appealingly simple wedge-like body. Even though he knew the wedge, or 'doorstop,' profile was not a very low-drag shape, Colin Chapman of Lotus adopted it as a foolproof means of holding the cars down to their correct ride height under all operating conditions at Indy. So right did these Lotuses look and so quickly did they go that their shape (which was only part of their formula for speed) was widely imitated in 1969 by the Indy gentry, many of whom are never happier than when they're building replicas of a successful car.

Rife though it was with original notions, the 1969 Eagle resembled the Lotus wedge in its basic body shape. Its engineering was entirely different, however — different also from all previous Eagles. In full charge of the design work on the new Eagle was Tony Southgate, the 28-year-old

Dan checks the progress of his new 1969 Indy Eagle with Pete Wilkins, Director of Fabrication for AAR. The car featured an exhaust system and valve spring retainers made from titanium.

Briton who had joined AAR at the end of 1967. Tony had been an assistant designer at Lola for five years, on projects including the Type 70 Group 7 car, and was at Brabham for a year before coming to AAR. His Brabham background showed particularly in the details of the '69 Eagle's front suspension, which had its upper wishbone braced to the rear and its lower wishbone braced more widely to the front, where its forward pivot was attached to the light tubular structure that also supported the low cross-flow radiator. The concentric springs and shock absorbers were placed outboard.

A low and wide monocoque was designed, flat-bottomed and nearly trapezoidal in cross-section, to keep the center of gravity of the fuel load as low as possible. It was planned to require an extra side tank to bring the fuel capacity up to the seventy-five-gallon limit so that the tank, wedge-profiled to match the body, could be put on the side of the car that was toward the inside of the track — on the left at Indy, or on the right at Riverside (obviously a different tank for each application).

All the fuel was carried forward of the firewall because the 1969 Eagle was of composite construction. From the firewall back the frame was tubular, composed of three steel tubes on each side, connected to a multi-tube arch above the clutch housing for the rear suspension attachments. This lightened the chassis and made it easier to adapt to the two different engines that would power the new cars: the turbocharged Ford and the Gurney Eagle Mark IV Ford. The inward-sloping ram pipes of the new Mark IV heads allowed them to be tucked into the space behind the headrest.

Pipes to and from the radiator were fitted into a chamfer at the lower right edge of the monocoque. Brakes were Airhearts, with ventilated discs, and the fifteen-inch wheels were ten inches wide in front and fourteen inches wide at the back, a new broader dimension allowed by USAC for the first time in 1969. Wheelbase was 3⅜ inches longer than before, at 99⅞ inches, and the overall length, including the ground-scraping beaked nose of fiberglass, was 167 inches. Weight was successfully kept moderate, at 1,440 pounds for the Eagle-powered car and 1,515 pounds for those with the heavier turbo-Ford.

The Brabham-like front suspension of the new Eagle-Santa Ana.

More detail of the new Eagle's left front suspension and Airheart disc brake.

None of these features attracted more attention on the day of the new car's debut than its striking lines. It was unveiled in AAR's home town, which proclaimed April 25, 1969 to be Dan Gurney Day, and in honor of which the '69 model was dubbed the Eagle-Santa Ana. It seemed to be one of the cleanest Indy cars ever conceived. A deep windscreen wrapped around the cockpit and flowed back to a high, curved headrest that tapered down to the tail, enclosing the engine inlet stacks. At the back its wedge shape rose to a tail cut off square at the rear edge of the rear wheels. So lovingly was the shape tailored for low drag that AAR had even built its own rear-view mirrors, faired into the sides of the screen.

Very late in starting, the 1969 AAR program yielded only four untested cars shortly before the month of May. A single bird left the nest, going to Smokey Yunick for a turbo-Ford engine. Joe Leonard drove it to sixth place in the race, in spite of having to make a pit stop for, of all things, a new radiator. He'd been second and challenging for first when a piece of track junk holed the core; that Yunick was able to get him back in the race to finish sixth is one clue to why they call Smokey's in Daytona Beach "The Best Damn Garage in Town."

Three views of the Eagle-Santa Ana entered at Indy in 1969 by Smokey Yunick. Left: The front view shows the wedge shape and slight offset of the front end. Middle: The white dial tells the all-important boost pressure from the turbo-Ford V-8 engine. Right: Joe Leonard drove the car to sixth place.

A similarly-powered Eagle-Santa Ana was driven by Denny Hulme, repeating from 1968 as Dan's teammate. He and Gurney were alternating in second and third places (Eagles at one point were placed 2-3-4-5) but Hulme was sidelined by clutch trouble on his last pit stop. Dan survived the 200 laps to place second in a car powered by the Gurney

Eagle engine. He had his choice of that and a twin with a turbo-Ford, but chose the unblown pushrod V-8 because it had shown the ability to run the distance the year before. Allowed by new USAC rules to be enlarged to 320 cubic inches, the engine had titanium exhaust headers. With refinements to the combustion chambers it produced 560 bhp on alcohol fuel and 580 bhp with a dash of nitro for qualifying.

The second-place finish came after one of the most exasperating months Gurney ever spent at the Speedway. The sleek unblown Santa Ana, which had been expected to reach 205 mph on the Indy straights, was struggling to exceed 175. Instead of being dramatically faster, it was no quicker than Dan's 1968 car. The team's desperate search for the reasons for the lack of speed was hampered by rainy weather, which sharply curtailed their time on the track. The faired engine cover was

The new, larger, 320-cid Gurney Eagle engine with Mark IV heads in Dan's car at Indy in 1969.

Gurney on his way to second place in the new Eagle at Indy in 1969; shown with Bobby Unser's (1) four-wheel-drive Lola powered by a turbo-Offy.

The right rear quarter, with oil cooler, of Denny Hulme's turbo-Ford AAR Eagle at Indy in 1969.

This view of the Smokey Yunick-entered 1969 Indy Eagle shows the very congested aerodynamic condition at the rear of the car.

stripped away; wire mesh replaced bodywork under the rear, and several different nose shapes were built and tried. Finally chosen was one with a frontal air inlet and an outlet duct aimed upward, instead of down and to the side. Even with these changes Dan was able to qualify only a fraction of a mile an hour faster than he had the year before.

After Indy, Dan's car was principally developed for use in the many road races that were on the USAC calendar in 1969, and there it obtained some commendable results. Gurney was second over 150 miles at Continental Divide Raceway, first in one of two one-hundred-mile races at Indianapolis Raceway Park, second overall in a two-heat race at Donnybrooke, and third in two events: the Rex Mays 300 at Riverside and the Dan Gurney 200 (named in his honor) at Seattle International Raceway. Dan finished the Rex Mays race with the drive to only one wheel work-

Dan completes a pit stop on his way to third place in Riverside's 1969 Rex Mays.

ing, after qualifying first and setting a new lap record so high that it stood for four years. In these last races the AAR crew experimented with wings of various types, small ones at the nose and athwart the engine cover. With the same car, Dan opened his 1970 season with a victory in another USAC road race at Sears Point in northern California.

The 1969 Eagle-Santa Ana was a car in advance of its time. Several years later Dan Gurney would say, "You know, that wasn't such a bad car." But it had blotted its copybook with its bad manners at Indy. In a manner that was not fully recognized at the time, the basic high-drag wedge shape had seemed to interact with the new wider rear tires to produce a virtual air brake at the rear end of the Eagle-Santa Ana. It had not been so damaging to the performance of the car with the more powerful turbo-Ford engine, but the effect had been pronounced on the weaker un-blown pushrod model. Later, through its experiments in USAC road racing and a successful test at Indy, AAR came to respect the ability and potential of the Santa Ana. But by that time the decision had long been made to design and build a completely new Eagle for the 1970 season.

At the time the 1969 Indy race was run Dan Gurney knew that Tony Southgate wouldn't be designing the 1970 car. Tony had accepted the post of chief designer for B.R.M., which he took up on June 22, 1969. Len Terry came to Indianapolis for the 1969 race, and there Gurney broached the idea of hiring Terry to design the 1970-model Eagle. Later Dan followed up with a firm commission. Terry flew to Santa Ana to talk over the design requirements and to get, from Phil Remington, drawings of some of the existing AAR hardware for possible incorporation into the new design. He was asked initially to shape it around the Offy engine, and after working three weeks in that direction in England AAR suggested that he make it adaptable to the turbo-Ford and the three-valve Gurney Eagle engine too — though the latter was never raced in one of these cars.

Again the AAR program was running late. Not until February, 1970, did Terry finish the drawings for the new car. He had sent prints to Gurney as he proceeded, so when he delivered the originals several weeks later he discovered, to his surprise, that parts for ten cars had been made and seven were being assembled. Dan would keep two, and the

The new Terry-designed 1970 chassis had rocker-type upper wishbones and a sloping radiator.

The dash panel of the 1970 Indy Eagle was mounted on six Lord rubber mounts to reduce the effects of vibration on the instruments.

others were to go to such drivers as Bobby Unser, Johnny Rutherford, Gordon Johncock and Lee Roy Yarbrough. This was the plan; the car did not live up to these high hopes.

The suspension linkages of the 1970 car featured upper wishbones that were sharply inclined downward toward the center of the car, at both front and rear, bringing with that a relatively low roll axis. At the front Terry kept the forward-braced lower wishbone layout of the '69 car while reaching back to his 1966 design for AAR to fit rocker-type upper wishbones, with inboard coil/shock units, to reduce aerodynamic drag.

Another reversion to 1966-68 practice was the use of a full-length monocoque frame. This allowed the full seventy-five-gallon fuel load to be carried in the frame, with no side tank. It also meant that the engine could not be relied on for an important part of the rear frame stiffness, as it was in the '69 Eagle, but in recompense the frequent engine changes that are part of life in Gasoline Alley could be carried out with less disturbance of the rear suspension geometry.

Skinned in 2024 T-4 aluminum, the monocoque had a very unusual shape. In plan view it resembled an arrowhead, widening from only twenty-five inches side-to-side at the front bulkhead to forty-eight inches just forward of the rear wheels. The monocoque itself reached full width at the firewall, bodywork being added from there to the rear to enclose the engine and suspension as much as possible. At the front a fiberglass nose housed an aluminum radiator sloped sharply forward — a favorite Terry technique — behind a venturi-shaped air inlet. The coolant pipes to and from the radiator were exposed on the upper side of the body, flanking the cockpit. Warm air leaving the radiator flowed upward over the surface of a triangular-section four-gallon engine oil tank and blew back over the screen and the driver, buffeting him in a storm of rough air at high speed.

The body-frame was also notable for its deeply curved underbelly and almost flat upper surface, a virtual inversion of the 1969 cross-section. Adoption of this shape was based on the AAR theory that the lack of speed of the '69 car was owed to a high-pressure 'cushion' of air forming beneath it; the curvature of the 1970 Eagle underside was provided to prevent the formation of this air cushion and to avoid front-end lift in the event that the nose of the car should rise under acceleration. Unfortunately, the shape also had the effect of raising the center of gravity of the laden Eagle.

Dan and others lobbied hard for a higher displacement limit (335 cid) for the unblown stock-block engine to keep it competitive in USAC racing. When this was rejected, he gave up on the Gurney Eagle Ford as a Speedway engine and turned to the turbocharged Drake Offy. He chose this instead of the turbo-Ford V-8 because it was less costly, was likely to need less development, was built very near their Santa Ana plant and was not distributed by arch-rival A.J. Foyt. Dan raced with a new short-stroke Offy of 4.28 × 2.75 inches that produced 725 bhp from its four cylinders in race tune and 800 bhp with a higher boost for qualifying. To save weight, Gurney used a two-speed LG200 Hewland gearbox.

These front and rear views of Gurney's 1970 Indy car, partially stripped of bodywork, show the radiator, oil tank and the turbo-Offy engine.

View of the new Eagle Sam Sessions drove to twelfth place at Indy in 1970.

Bobby Unser's Indy Eagle with Ford turbo power in 1970. He elected to race 1967 Eagle instead.

Sam Posey failed to qualify this Vatis-owned, modified early Eagle at Indy in 1970. This was Gurney's 1966 car.

Off to a late start to begin with, the 1970 program was further delayed when the first new cars were assembled. Though built to Terry's drawings, they had far too little total wheel travel at the rear. "It required a lot of time-consuming modification just to commence the testing," Dan Gurney recalled. "It was grim." And that was only the beginning. At the Indy Speedway the new Eagles didn't handle well. The high center of gravity and low roll axis seemed to combine to make them dodgy in the turns unless they were very stiffly sprung—which then provoked other quirks. Bobby Unser rejected his new car and drove a 1967 Eagle instead. The only new Eagle other than Dan's to qualify was a turbo-Ford-powered car turned down by Lee Roy Yarbrough; driven by Sammy Sessions, it was the slowest car in the field, placing twelfth in the race.

Dan with the new turbo-Offy Eagle he drove to third place at Indy in 1970.

Gurney had no choice but to persevere with his own car. He and his crew got better results with a raised ride height, which brought with it a higher roll axis. Yet Dan's qualifying speed was only 166.860 mph, just a flick of a stopwatch needle from his speed of 166.512 mph in 1968 with some 300 less horsepower! Starting from the fourth row he put in what he later called "one of my better drives against the odds." He made eleven pit stops as he battled handling troubles and fuel exhaustion to eke out a third-place finish. This would have been fine for most racers but it was a disaster for Dan, who had been tipped as the early favorite to win after placing second two years in a row.

As in 1969, this Eagle had been too new and too little tested to give of its best at Indy. AAR would develop it further, and it would have to, for the company had such an investment in cars built to the Len Terry design that it had to get as much out of them as possible. And in the business slow-down of 1970-71, sponsors eager to back the building of all-new racing cars were rare indeed.

AAR tested and then tested again, and when the first race was held on California's new Ontario Motor Speedway on Labor Day, 1970, the Eagle had been utterly transformed. It sprouted short wings just ahead of the rear wheels and stub wings at the front as well, refinements that helped Dan Gurney circulate this Indy-like track at an average of 176.4 mph to qualify second-fastest. He ran a strong second in the 500-mile race, then took the lead. Confusion at a pit stop dropped him back but he rose again to third place at half-distance, when an oil line broke, sprayed a tire and spun him into a wall. One would have wished Dan better luck, for this was his last race in an Eagle. Later he announced his retirement from competition at the age of 39, a decision on which he has, happily, never reneged.

Gurney closed the '70 season as team manager in a 150-mile USAC race at Phoenix on November 21. Making his debut in the cockpit of an AAR Eagle was Bobby Unser, who led until he broke in the ex-Gurney machine. Also in the field was Swede Savage in a 1970 Eagle with a Gurney Eagle Ford pushrod engine. Sensationally, Swede won the race on the last lap with this Eagle, which had been

Bobby Unser's Eagle-Offy next to Johnny Rutherford's modified earlier-model Eagle-Offy—about to take the green flag at the start of the Phoenix 1971 Jimmy Bryan 150.

fitted with long, sloping aerodynamic ramps extending from the sides of the cockpit all the way to the tail. By now the upper surfaces of the cars had been cleaned up by the relocation of the pipes to and from the water radiator.

Swede's tuneup for this victory had been a tire test session earlier in November in this same car at Indianapolis, where the more elaborate aerodynamic ramps were first tried. Wool tufts taped to the body helped the crew study the flow of air over the ramps and also over two wings placed low, just behind the front wheels. These low flank wings remained a distinctive feature of the Eagles through the 1971 season, in the early months of which the cars showed excellent speed.

Dan helps refuel Bobby Unser's Eagle at the first race of the 1971 season in Phoenix. Painted on the car are graphics reading: "The Available Eagle" and "This Car For Hire Contact Dan Gurney."

From the basic 1970 components two new cars were prepared for Indy in 1971. They had the low side wings and a wing built into the bodywork just above the engine. Bobby Unser qualified one on the front row at 175.81 mph, topped in speed only by the new M15 McLarens. With Savage laid up after an accident, the other new car was given to Lee Roy Yarbrough, who demolished it in a practice crash. A backup car — the one Swede had driven late in 1970 and early in 1971, now with an Offy engine — was hastily readied and given to Jim Malloy, who put it in the field at an excellent 171.83 mph and was the highest-placed AAR and Eagle driver after 500 miles, in fourth place. Bobby's car was strongly in contention, leading the race for a total of twenty-one laps, until he had to spin off the track, hitting a wall, to avoid another driver's accident.

That was the story of All American Racers and the Eagle-Offy in 1971: Boosted by expensive AAR development work on the Offy, Bobby Unser showed big speed, then broke. He won the pole position and/or set new track records in seven of the ten races on the USAC schedule, but won only twice, in the Trenton 300 and the Milwaukee 200. He set the fastest lap ever officially recorded on a recognized race track by winning the pole for the Michigan 200 at 193.444 mph. He and Swede Savage qualified second and fourth for the September 500 at Ontario, but in the race had trouble with new wing arrays. Both cars had wings at the nose, ahead of the front wheels, and high, full-width wings at the rear of the chassis.

Regarded by observers as merely imitative of the new McLarens, these Eagle wings at Ontario were actually gathering on-track data for one of the most important features of the all-new Eagle that was already being built for 1972. AAR's speed record in 1971 had been prodigious, but it would be utterly eclipsed by the car that was then being assembled in that unmarked building in Santa Ana.

Eagles Fly

The Eagle was born in 1966. It came of age in 1972. All that had gone before was adolescence. On its way to maturity the Eaglet had done some remarkable things, including winning Indy in 1968. Looking back from the vantage point of 1972 we saw that that was a precocious teen-age prank. In '72 the mature bird shook off its molting feathers and spread its wings. This, we could now see, was the real Eagle. This was the car Dan Gurney had meant to build all along.

As earlier chapters have illustrated, it is not easy to build a racing car. The final product is an amalgam of ideas, hunches, prejudices, pet notions, calculations and emotions. The severe pressures of time that are endemic to auto racing usually prevent the achievement of an 'ideal' or minimum-compromise design solution. By breaking the annual sequence of events, however, AAR succeeded in escaping from those time pressures. By continuing to race a developed 1970 Eagle in 1971, AAR's executives and engineers gained the time needed to begin early on an all-new car for 1972. In April, 1972, Dan Gurney would be able to say, "We are further along on our development program than we have been in five years."

At the heart of this program during the latter half of 1971 was AAR's chief designer, 31-year-old Roman Slobodynskyj. Born in Ukrania, Roman came to the U.S. at the age of nine. After some college training he became a draftsman and then a designer in one of the aerospace operations of the North American Rockwell Corporation. Meanwhile,

Eagle designer Roman Slobodynskyj.

Roman built a car of his own design to compete in the SCCA's D sports-racing class. This intensified his interest in cars, which inevitably led him to contact AAR. He did some part-time work for them in 1967, helping them design a dynamometer gearbox, and then joined AAR full-time in January, 1969 at Gurney's invitation. Drafting components for the new cars, he became familiar with the work of Southgate on the '69 Eagle and then of Terry on the 1970 car. Dan and his associates thought well enough of Slobodynskyj's work to promote him from within to the post of chief designer in May, 1971. This recognized the contributions he'd made to the much-improved 1971 Eagle.

The direct inspiration for the 1972 Eagle was the high speed shown by the 1971 McLaren USAC car, the M16. That, said Dan Gurney, lit "a

Made to last: The front end of the new Eagle chassis, Indy, 1972.

very hot fire under us." Before the race team went east to compete at Indy the subject of a new car had been thoroughly discussed at Santa Ana and, with Roman's appointment, design work had begun. The first drawing of a part for the new car, a rear suspension upright, was dated May 27, 1971. By July a consulting firm, Developmental Sciences, had used the well-calibrated GALCIT wind tunnel to check the aerodynamic characteristics of a simple one-tenth scale model of the planned new Eagle. Working with Slobodynskyj on its details were designer Dick Lindhurst and engineer Gary Wheeler.

Gurney and his design staff took full advantage of the changes in USAC rules for 1972. They moved the outside wheel edges out to the full permissible eighty-inch maximum width. By so doing they provided the

The variable-length right-hand arm of the Eagle's rear anti-roll bar for in-race adjustments. This AAR 1972 Indy entry has a Weismann transaxle.

greatest possible span for the front and rear wings, which, like any other part of the body, may extend no farther than the vertical planes that connect the centers of the front and rear tires on each side of the car. They also moved the rear edge of the rear wing back to the maximum forty-two-inch distance from the rear-wheel centerline, and placed the wing as high as possible, thirty-two inches (formerly the limit was twenty-eight inches) above the bottom of the chassis tub. The new car's overall length was the maximum allowed by the rules, fifteen feet, and its wheelbase was six inches longer than the minimum at 102 inches.

Combined in the structure of the 1972 Eagle were the best ideas culled from the 1969 and 1970-71 models. The frame design resembled that of the 1969 Eagle-Santa Ana in that the Offy engine was used as part

Beautiful work: The left-hand radiator of the new Eagle at Indy in 1972. Nearby is the fuel-valve control lever.

of the structure from the firewall back. On each side of the engine four supplementary steel tubes converged to attachment points low at the sides of the clutch housing. Bolted thereto and to the transaxle were a sheet steel bridge and tubular braces to the rear suspension and wing. The rollover bar was affixed to the front end of the engine.

Bulkheads of square steel tubing formed the skeleton to which the SAE 2024 aluminum skin of the main monocoque was riveted. This was a wide, flat 'tub' which, except for its narrow cockpit, looked at first glance like the frame of a sports-racing car. The leading ends of the side boxes were beveled inward toward the front, changing direction and heading straight forward again at the dash line. Behind the dash a sheet aluminum tetrahedron added stiffness to the frame above the driver's knees. His

The John Miller-prepared AAR short-stroke Offy in Bobby Unser's Eagle at Indy, 1972.

Two views of the reassuringly work-manlike cockpit of Bobby Unser's 1972 Eagle-Offy. Beneath the steering column (upper photo) is the selector valve for the anti-roll bar adjusting system. And left of the steering wheel is the lever to change the fuel tank feeding valve.

feet rested in the box at the front of the monocoque that recalled the 1970 Eagle design, with sturdy mounts for the pivots of rocker-type upper wishbones and space for inboard-mounted coil/shock assemblies and an anti-roll bar. The Schroeder rack and pinion steering, mounted behind the suspension, provided a 16:1 overall ratio and two turns lock to lock.

Drawing on all AAR's experience, the suspension geometry was planned with special care. Its Goodyear connections helped AAR gain a jump on its competitors in the utilization of that company's new 1972 tires, the first to be run at Indy with no tread pattern at all. The wheels were little changed, of fifteen-inch diameter and ten- and fourteen-inch width at front and rear. Also carried over from the 1970-71 Eagles were the front uprights with 'live' hubs and the Airheart disc brakes, with 12.2-inch ventilated rotors. Rectangular-section scoops fed air to the front brakes for racing. The scoops were removed for qualifying, since the brakes didn't get hot enough in four laps to require cooling.

Inside the new Eagle's low nose were the brake- and clutch-fluid reservoirs, battery, fire extinguisher, two-way radio (if fitted), and a tubular steel structure that carried to the chassis the downforce from the two adjustable front wings. Made by Camber, Inc., the fiberglass nose was shaped to divert as much air as possible up and over the top of the car. Below lips overhanging each side of the nose, air flowed back from the wings to small ducts, to cool the Monroe shock absorbers, and then through the suspension to the radiators. Tucked into the beveled front corners of the monocoque frame, the radiators had special angled cores to suit the air flow from the coarse-screened inlet to the special fiberglass duct at the side outlet.

The 1972 Eagle's broad flanks enclosed the tanks for seventy-five U.S. gallons of fuel. These were connected to the fuel system by a selector valve that allowed the driver to choose which tank to use first. No bodywork was fitted or even intended from the firewall back, the AAR men valuing highly the cooling effect of airflow around the hard-working Offy engine. In this Offy John Miller used the short-stroke dimensions of 4.38 × 2.65 inches, with grooved and lightened pistons made to his design by Drake Engineering. AAR Offy engines also had special short connecting rods and crankcases built, by Drake, to their order with two oil scavenge pumps instead of the usual single pump. John Miller found that this pump arrangement, which was an AAR exclusive until April, 1973, gave a measurable increase in horsepower.

American-made, four-speed Weismann transaxles were used in the new AAR Eagles and in some of those raced by customers; others used the Hewland LG-series units. Below the drive half-shafts there were two lateral links to each hub carrier, with a single link above and the usual two trailing radius rods. Used on the AAR cars and optional to customers (above the base price of $25,550) was a system developed during 1971 to allow the driver to vary the stiffness of the rear anti-roll bar, and hence the steer characteristics of the car, while it was under way. This system consisted of a right-hand lever arm for the bar that was made of a hydraulic cylinder and piston. By using a pump between his legs, and a selector valve under the steering column, the driver could lengthen or shorten that arm at will.

This new Eagle was no lightweight. In race-ready form its dry weight was 1,540 pounds, 190 above the USAC minimum. Gurney, Remington, Slobodynskyj and Bobby Unser were, however, quite happy to have a fast oval-track racer that was also uncompromisingly strong. "If you are going to race," said Dan, "it must be *strong* over *light* if you cannot have both." The weight was placed extremely low. At long last, this was the ultra-low racer Dan Gurney had wanted to build since he set up AAR. Its weight was distributed sixty percent to the rear, not a large amount by modern racing car standards. It was so apportioned to match the legally-limited sizes of the tires on the front and rear wheels. Unless the rear wings were extremely effective, a greater weight on the rear tires tended to cause handling problems at the high speeds being reached on the super-speedways (Indianapolis, Ontario, Michigan and a new track at Pocono in Pennsylvania.)

Speaking of effective wings, this is just what the new Eagle had. The downswept nose, the low-profile fuel tanks, the smooth upper body surfaces, the very narrow cockpit, the slim and tucked-in Offy engine and even the ogival rear-view mirrors added up to the most intense effort yet made by any builder to ensure that the wide rear wing received a clear and effective flow of air. At the car's peak Indy speed, about 210 mph, front and rear wings together were capable of generating as much additional downforce as the car's dry weight: some 1,550 pounds. With the new Goodyear slick tires, this was enough to carry Bobby Unser through the Indy turns at better than 181 mph on his fastest laps.

The original new Eagle, no. 7201, first turned a wheel at Ontario Motor Speedway on December 10, 1971. It soon proved it had been born for speed. Some features had to be changed, of course. A camber-controlling linkage on the rear suspension was tried, but judged not helpful. A large NASA duct in the nose for cockpit air was too big, so was soon blocked off. A scoop on the left rear of the monocoque for the engine-oil radiator was moved, before the car raced, from the side to the top of the body. Running on 1971 tires, however, the unpainted new Eagle was lapping Ontario at 192 mph, 5 mph faster than the record. And with the new tires, Bobby Unser astounded the world of racing with a timed 196.9 mph lap during Goodyear tire testing there in March, 1972.

If potential buyers had been sitting on the fence before, this flaunting of sheer speed soon tipped them off into the Eagle camp. Unser underlined it with an Indy test lap at 190.8 mph in late March and a victory in the Phoenix 150 to open the 1972 USAC season. This was in the original prototype, 7201, which served as the AAR backup car for Indy. Seven more cars were made before the 1972 Indy 500, two of them (numbers 7203 and 7205) being kept for AAR's own use. Another new Eagle, number 7206, was the fastest machine on the Indiana track for the first seven days of May in the hands of Jim Malloy, who had driven so well for AAR in 1971. But then Jim crashed heavily during a practice run and was killed. Gurney and his technicians checked the wreckage with unusual care in an attempt to satisfy themselves, which they did, that the accident was almost certainly not caused by a major failure in what was, after all, a still-new Eagle car design.

With the new treadless tires and the wider wings allowed, all thirty-three cars in the 1972 field qualified faster than the highest speed of 1971 (178.696 mph, Peter Revson, in a McLaren). Bobby Unser's Eagle was

Mister Speed at Indy: Bobby Unser's spectacular Eagle in qualifying trim (only one mirror and the wings steeply angled for maximum downforce).

Bobby Unser and Dan Gurney at Indy in 1972.

the fastest of all at a stunning 195.940 mph average with a fastest lap (of four) of 196.678 mph. This gave both Bobby and AAR their first pole-position start at Indy, an honor fought for and respected almost as much as victory in the race itself. Unser also dominated the early running of the race but retired after thirty-one laps with the most picayune fault imaginable: a broken distributor rotor. In the other AAR car, painted purple and dubbed the 'Mystery Eagle,' Jerry Grant was leading in the late stages of the race but lost that lead when he had to pit unexpectedly to change a tire. Because a crewman erroneously plugged a fuel hose from Bobby Unser's tank into the Mystery Eagle it was demoted from second to

Car owner Ken Norris, Jr. (left) and chief mechanic Jack McCormack are seen with the Eagle-Offy driven to fifth place at Indy in 1972 by Sam Posey.

Weird: Antares-modified nose of Swede Savage's 1970-model Eagle at Indy in 1972.

twelfth place in the final standings, a difference of $70,000 in prize money. The only other new Eagle running at the flag was Sam Posey's, in fifth place.

Engine troubles also kept Bobby Unser from finishing in the other two 500-mile races in 1972. They knew he'd been there, however; he cut an unprecedented swath of speed through USAC's Championship Trail. He captured the pole position in seven of the ten USAC races, led more laps (520) than any of his competitors, and won more races (four) than any other driver on the trail. Indy qualifying was the first of three occasions on which he bettered his own world closed-circuit speed record originally set at Michigan International Speedway in 1971. The second time was again at MIS — 199.889 mph — and the third at Ontario at 201.965 mph. At the latter track he did not gain the pole, however, for he ran the day after Jerry Grant had seized that honor with an average of 199.600 mph and a first lap at 201.414 mph, making Grant and his Eagle-Offy the first in history to turn an officially-timed lap at better than 200 mph in USAC competition.

At Ontario the AAR Eagles had been given new front and rear suspension components that widened the car's track by two and three inches

Dick Simon (44) in a 1972 Eagle with the 1973 update kit powered by a turbocharged V-8 Ford engine at Phoenix in 1973.

at the front and rear respectively, bringing those dimensions to sixty-five and sixty-one inches. For the '73 season AAR sold parts kits to update earlier Eagles to the wider track; these parts were also used in the new cars they built and sold to the basic 1972 design. To meet the tremendous demand they built two batches of new cars, nine more before the end of 1972 and an additional eight before Indy in 1973. Thus, twenty of the thirty-three starters at Indy in 1973 were Dan Gurney's Eagles. Three had Foyt-Ford V-8 engines and one of these, that of Mel Kenyon, placed fourth. First and second places in the 1973 500 (shortened by rain to 332½ miles) were taken by new 1972-model Eagle-Offys. One early-1972 Eagle, entered by Smokey Yunick, qualified with a turbocharged Chevrolet engine but did not race with the leaders.

For its own 1973 entries AAR built a new model that represented a refinement in every detail of the 1972 machine. It was hard to improve on

Two views of Indy's 1973 winning car: a 1972-model Eagle that was driven by Gordon Johncock. The special front tire fairings were added by chief mechanic George Bignotti.

A flock of Eagles at Indy in 1973: Jerry Grant accompanies his AAR Eagle-Offy (48), Mark Donohue in his Eagle-Offy, Wally Dallenbach's AAR Eagle-Offy (62), David Hobbs' Black Label Eagle (73).

such a masterpiece. As Dan Gurney said when he brought the new car to Ontario for tests in mid-February, "We hope we haven't slowed it down too much!" The new track dimensions were used, now with a greater lateral distance between the suspension pivot points. Instead of being tapered inward toward the rear, in plan view, the frame tub was widened about three inches at the back so its sides would be parallel. This addition allowed the whole tub to be made lower and shallower from top to bottom, without a loss in fuel capacity, a change that brought both a further reduction in the height of the center of gravity and an increase in the flow of free air to the rear wing.

Bill Vukovich took second place at Indy in 1973 with this 1972-type Eagle with a Hewland gearbox and upswept Offy inlet manifold.

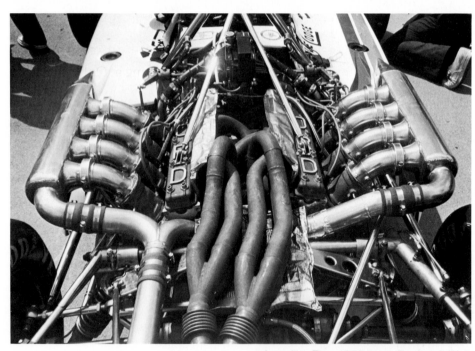

A rarity: The 1972-type Eagle of Dick Simon with a turbocharged Ford V-8 engine at Indianapolis in 1973.

Aerodynamics were improved in detail. Airflow to the two coolant radiators was made smoother by reshaping the sides of the nose, and new slotted wings were developed for both the front and rear by Gary Wheeler and a McDonnell-Douglas aerodynamicist, Bob Liebeck, for whom the new wing was named. Resembling the inverted form of an airfoil used on aircraft built to land slowly and take off steeply, the wing's added effectiveness was more evident on slower one-mile tracks than it was on the super-speedways. Reduced drag at the rear of the car might have resulted from another change that was tried only in brief pre-season tests: inlet and exhaust manifolds curved downward so the whole turbocharging system could be set lower, reducing the height of the center of gravity and taking some of the lumpy objects out of the airflow.

Close-up of the rear wing design on the new 1973-model Eagle.

The fuel tank layout was revised on the 1973 Eagle to gain improved control over the manner in which the methanol was consumed. A more rugged mounting for the fire extinguisher bottle was devised. After the first of the new cars was demolished during testing at Ontario in mid-March (Bobby Unser escaping miraculously), the roll-over bar was affixed to the monocoque instead of the engine. Roman Slobodynskyj and his crew had worked hard to reduce weight. Ready to race, the later 1973 cars weighed between 1,450 and 1,500 pounds. Three more cars of the 1973 series were made for AAR's USAC campaign, plus two additional cars that were sold to other teams in July, bringing the total production of this Eagle model to six.

AAR's sales success was not matched by its accomplishments on the tracks in 1973. Bobby Unser led for a total of 424 racing laps, 103 more than his nearest rival, but managed to be in the lead at the end of a USAC race only once: a 150-mile race at Milwaukee in June. He had led, at one time or another, in ten other races in his Olsonite Eagle during 1973. As usual the Unser Eagle qualified spectacularly. It was clocked at 204.487 mph at MIS and at 212.766 mph at Texas World Speedway, where Bobby was timed at 203 mph on his second lap and averaged 200.551 mph for the first forty miles — before retiring with a broken piston.

The limited-production 1973 Eagle served as the pattern for the 1974 model, of which a dozen complete examples were delivered

A. J. Watson's improvements to the nose of a 1968 Eagle for Mike Mosley at Indy in 1973.

Bobby Unser's 1973 AAR Eagle, the
same car in which he previously set a
closed course world speed record.

Bobby Unser at speed in the 1974 Eagle-Offy (compare the subtle differences between this model and the photo of '73's).

Bobby Unser in the winner's circle at the Ontario Motor Speedway—where he won the 1974 California 500.

between January 11 and February 28, 1974. Conforming with a change in USAC rules that took place during 1973, each carried only forty U.S. gallons of fuel, all on the left-hand side of the chassis. The tubs of the new cars were subtly reshaped to allow the radiators and their ducting to be shifted rearward, helping to ease the flow of air around the front wheels. On AAR's own Eagles, wide aprons appeared inboard of the front wheels. They formed an outward extension of the area of the underbody of the car from the nose to the radiators.

To reduce speeds USAC mandated narrower rear wings in 1974 (as well as smaller total fuel allotments in each race), so the '74 Eagle had an even narrower cockpit to preserve the best possible air flow over the smaller wing. Gone was the long rearward brace for the roll-over bar, which now had two shorter braces to the frame just behind the cockpit. This was a recognition feature of the 1974 Eagle, as was the use of triangular instead of rectangular rubber inserts in the nose panel to give

Aerodynamic forces on front wings and nose are evident in this rare photo of the 1974 Eagle at speed on the Indy main straight. Rear tires are also much higher than when at rest, expanded by centrifugal force.

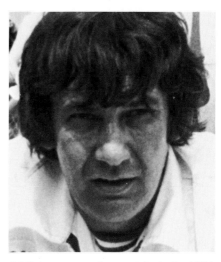

AAR team members at Indy in 1974: engine man John Miller (top) and chief mechanic Wayne Leary (bottom).

99

The unique box around the engine oil cooler on Bobby Unser's 1974 Eagle; it ducted the warm air out and upward.

clearance for the inner ends of the front rocker-type wishbones when the wheels were extended to the rebound limit.

AAR was paid the supreme compliment by one of its arch-rivals in 1974. Vel's-Parnelli Jones Racing, which had been building special cars for Mario Andretti and Al Unser since 1972, bought three of the new Eagles to race in the '74 season. In the California 500 at Ontario in March, the first USAC race of the year, Bobby Unser won his first 500-mile event since 1968 and edged his brother Al's Eagle by only 0.58 seconds for the

Bobby Unser, Ozzie Olson and Dan Gurney at Michigan International Speedway.

victory. This set the pace for the season, one in which A.J. Foyt won the pole positions but Bobby Unser — at last — collected the finishes and the championship points.

Only once in '74 did Bobby's Eagle fail to finish. He won the California 500, the Trenton 200, the Michigan 200 and the Trenton 300. He was second five times: Indianapolis, two 150-mile races at Phoenix, a one-hundred-mile qualifying race at Ontario and the first 150-mile heat of the Trenton 300. He gained a fourth place in the Milwaukee 200 and a fifth in the Pocono 500. His placings in the three 500-mile races won Bobby the 1974 Triple Crown Championship. Even more important was the grand total of USAC points that gave Bobby Unser his second USAC National Driving Championship.

Bobby Unser (48) and Gordon Johncock (20) racing their 1974-model Eagles at Phoenix in November, 1974. They finished one-two, in the reverse of the order shown here.

Team portrait of the U.S. Auto Club
1974 National Champions. Left to right:
Dean Williams, Butch Wilson, Bobby
Boxx, Wayne Leary, Bobby Unser and
Dan Gurney.

Just as it had in 1970, auto racing in America suffered in 1975 from a sharp business recession. Several major sponsors were forced to curtail their backing or drop out of racing altogether; among them was Ozzie Olson, staunch supporter of Dan Gurney and the Eagles for so long. It was one of those bitter ironies of auto racing that Olson should give up his sponsorship of AAR just a few months before the team scored its most prized victory, its 1975 win at Indianapolis. The name on the side of the triumphant Eagle was new but still Scandinavian: Jorgensen.

From an initial association with AAR in 1972, the involvement of the Earle M. Jorgensen Company grew into full-fledged sponsorship of Dan Gurney's USAC campaign in 1975. Earle Jorgensen, who founded his firm in the twenties, was still its chairman and chief executive when the link with AAR was made. This came about because AAR was buying many of the metals it needed from the Los Angeles branch of Jorgensen, which makes steels and forgings, and distributes steel and aluminum. As it does in racing, one thing led to another and Jorgensen found itself an enthusiastic backer of Gurney's own Eagle racing program.

Since its support was split between AAR's efforts in both USAC and Formula 5000 (see Chapter 6), Jorgensen had to agree to a sharp cutback in the number of Gurney's entries on the USAC Championship Trail. They focused on the three big 500-mile races, the first of which was held on a chilly, overcast March 9, at Ontario Motor Speedway. The driver was Bobby Unser and the car was the well-proven 1974 Eagle-Offy, now in the light blue Jorgensen colors and bearing the traditional Gurney number 48 instead of the numeral 1 that USAC Champion Unser could have worn. The Eagle looked much as it had in 1974 except for the addition of much deeper tip fences, the plates that help control air flow, on the all-important rear wing.

Bobby Unser showed his mastery of the Eagle and the Ontario track by qualifying for the California 500 with two laps that were identical right down to the third decimal point: 194.554 mph. That was almost nine mph faster than his speed on the same track the year before and was good enough to put him in the center of the front row for the start. Bobby had bad luck in a one-hundred-mile preliminary race, retiring after sixty miles with piston failure, but had some good fortune in reserve for the main event. Unser's Eagle placed second, 43.33 seconds back of the Foyt Coyote that dominated most of the stops on the Championship Trail in 1975. They were both three laps ahead of the rest of the field. One Eagle victory was put on the board at Ontario: Wally Dallenbach's in a one-hundred-mile race in a car prepared by George Bignotti.

Ontario proved to be a beautiful tuneup for Indy for the AAR team. There they left the pre-race speed duels to Foyt and Johncock, concentrating instead on the search for better fuel economy, but when qualifying was over the light blue AAR car was in perfect position: on the outside of the front row. Bobby put it into the show with a best lap of 191.327 mph and a four-lap qualifying average of 191.073 mph. That made him the fastest of the sixteen Eagles that made the 1975 Indy field, by far

Bobby Unser leads the 1975 California 500 in his Eagle; he finished second.

the largest share of the thirty-three starters enjoyed by any car maker. Like Bobby's own mount they were all carried over from 1974 and earlier campaigns, for AAR built no new USAC cars for the 1975 season.

The Bobby Unser Eagle was not one of the challengers for the lead in the early laps of the 500 on May 25. Instead the team was nursing its 280-gallon fuel allotment to be sure it would have enough to be running fast at the finish. Bobby was not far off the pace, though, running second and third through the first half of the race and taking the lead for just one lap on lap 124. A little later, on his seventh pit stop on lap 130, Bobby was given more boost from his Offy's turbo-supercharger so he'd be able to maneuver better in traffic.

Unser took the lead again on lap 165 when Johnny Rutherford made a pit stop. He was still leading when storm clouds appeared, seemingly out of nowhere, and it began to sprinkle during the 173rd lap of the leaders. On lap 174 Bobby rushed into the pits under the yellow caution light for a quick ten-second fill-up of fuel, his eleventh stop of the race. This "was to make sure I had enough fuel so I could race hard the rest of the way," Bobby said afterward. But there was no more racing that day. The black clouds split open and drenched the track, sending cars spinning and sliding on their smooth-treaded tires. Bobby kept his blue Eagle pointed straight as he crossed the finish line with Dan Gurney's jubilant voice in his ears over the pit-to-car radio: "This is it! We won!"

That *was* it — Bobby Unser's second Eagle-mounted win at Indy and the first victory there, in the tenth year of trying, for a car built and entered by All American Racers. The red flag had fallen on the 175th lap and the race was scored as of the positions on the 174th, after 435 miles, which showed Unser in the lead with a margin of a minute and four seconds ahead of Rutherford's McLaren. It was a wet but welcome triumph for the men from Santa Ana.

The rest of the '75 season was anticlimactic. Gearbox trouble dropped Bobby out of the other premier event, the Schaefer 500 at Pocono, and he broke a kneecap in a crash in another team's Eagle at Michigan International Speedway in September. Bobby Unser finished fifth in an AAR Eagle entry in another race at the Michigan track, and

(Overleaf) Having won the 1975 Indianapolis 500, Bobby Unser drove his Eagle-Offy to second place at Milwaukee two weeks later.

placed second at Milwaukee just after Indy, collecting enough points in these events to end the year in third place in the USAC Championship standings.

At season's end Bobby and Dan agreed, without rancor or recrimination, to go their separate ways. Mechanics Wayne Leary and Butch Wilson went with Bobby, and Dean Williams retired from race car wrenching. Dan signed the 1974 USAC sprint car champion, Duane Carter, Jr., to drive his Eagles on the Championship Trail in 1976.

Looking back on his five-year association with Bobby Unser, Dan Gurney said, "I hope our old team will be remembered for its accomplishments. The records speak for themselves." They certainly do. So did the $214,031 that Bobby collected for winning the Indianapolis 500. When it came his turn at the Indy victory dinner, Bobby Unser asked that everyone present who had contributed to his victory come up to the head table to be recognized. Some two dozen crew members came forward to blink gratefully in the unaccustomed limelight next to Unser. It was a generous gesture by a driver big enough to be able to admit that he rode to victory on the shoulders of many men and women. Like Dan Gurney, Bobby Unser is obviously "a man who knows how to win."

Bobby Unser, winner of the 1975 Indianapolis 500, his second victory at the 'Brickyard.'

⑥ Return to the Road

Jerry Grant, that burly, balding racer from the Pacific Northwest, crops up in every chapter of the Eagle saga. No stranger to speed, Jerry could be counted on to probe any new car design to its limits. That's why he was nominated by Dan Gurney to be the first to drive a completely new car from AAR. This was a dual-purpose machine, conceived for both Formula 5000 and Formula 1, and its baptismal trial was at Riverside in August, 1973. It did not race, however, until June 2, 1974. No other Eagle had to wait so long to be given a chance to prove what it could do.

This new Eagle was to mark AAR's return to Formula 5000, which had been known as Formula A when the company last built cars to suit it in 1968-69. The formula rules still required the use of stock American block and head components in a five-liter V-8 engine, so AAR planned it to suit Chevrolet, Ford and American Motors engines, the only ones its potential customers were likely to want to use. The design was also made adaptable to the three-liter Cosworth-Ford V-8 so this new Eagle road-racer could compete in Formula 1, for which it would have had its fuel capacity increased from thirty to fifty U.S. gallons. No such Grand Prix versions of the 1974 model were actually built, however.

Dan's Slobodynskyj/Wheeler/Lindhurst team began designing the new car during the 1972-73 winter, and construction proceeded into the spring and early summer as the greater demands of the Indy car manufacturing program allowed. Those craftsmen most closely associated with the assembly of the F.5000 Eagle were Dave Klym and Bobby

Boxx. The car they put together could not belie its hereditary relationship to the fabulously fast 1972 USAC Eagle. It had the same flat, downcurving nose with wings, the same wide flanks with leading-edge radiators, and the same big, high wing at the rear. But from nose to tail this was an entirely new machine. Such had been the rate of progress in both USAC and Formula 5000 that it seemed no longer possible to make one chassis concept work for both, as AAR had done in 1968.

As in the USAC machine, the flank-mounted twin coolant radiators were a hallmark of the Formula 5000 design. The smaller fuel capacity requirement of F.5000 allowed the ducts to and from the radiators to be much deeper, carving into the sides of the monocoque, which in plan view widened in a bell-shape toward its broad back end. From the firewall of the aluminum-skinned frame rearward, the structure was provided by tubular bracing and the engine itself, a Chevrolet V-8 modified by John Miller.

At its front end the frame was one of the most complex AAR had ever made. Its monocoque toebox was at the center of a network of square-section steel tubes extending to the left and right to carry the pivot points for the front suspension wishbones. This left room for one of the new Eagle's main innovations: inboard-mounted front disc brakes. Connected to the live front hubs by universal-jointed shafts, the brakes were frame-mounted to keep the unsprung weight, that of the wheel and tire assemblies, as light as possible. Placed inboard at both front and rear, the ventilated discs were 10.15 inches in diameter, 0.94 inch thick and gripped by Airheart calipers.

A rocker-type upper wishbone was again used at the front, so the coil/shock units could be mounted inboard for aerodynamic reasons. To keep those springs out of the way of the brakes, however, the rockers were cranked so that they and their concentric shock absorbers could be placed to the rear of the discs. The rear suspension was similar to that of the USAC Eagle, hung from bracketry around the Hewland DG300 transaxle. British-made Melmag wheels were fitted. Very light, made of sheet magnesium with a honeycomb core, they had a thirteen-inch diameter and eleven-inch rim width in front and fifteen-inch diameter and seventeen-inch width in the rear.

The inboard brake mounting contributed to the attainment of another of the design goals of the F. 5000 Eagle: tucking as much weight as possible well within the track and wheelbase to reduce its moment of inertia around the car's vertical axis, so it would be more willing to take turns. Ducts in the nosepiece took air to and from the inboard discs. Two engine oil radiators were mounted just back of the rear edge of the monocoque, and received air through scoops in the upper surfaces of the fiberglass body. There was no transparent windscreen and, as on the Eagle-Santa Ana, the upper portion of the engine room was fully enclosed. An oval scoop drew in air for the engine's induction system. As new regulations required, the side portions of the body were built to provide controlled crush-resistance to protect the driver in a crash.

The first of this new breed of Eagle was raw and unpainted when it rolled out at Riverside in the heat of August, 1973. The temperature was high enough to reveal that the engine wasn't happy with its cooling system, so test runs were made in bursts of four or five laps until, after many weeks' work, many small improvements in concert brought the overheating under control. By this time New Englander Sam Posey, a potential customer for one of these $40,000 Eagles, had taken over the test-driving role. Front-wheel offset was reduced, cutting the track from sixty-five to sixty-three inches, to cure a tendency to weave left and right on the pavement. A lack of braking power was traced to overcooling of the front linings, and was remedied by reducing their ration of cool air.

After this first phase of testing, which ended in October, the new Eagle's beak was radically reworked with the help of the AAR consultant on aerodynamics, Bob Liebeck. The original design had been like that of the USAC Eagle, right down to the little flared apron around its underside that was intended to keep air from slipping under the car when the nose dived under braking. The new nosepiece kept the slotted side wings and added a central wing built into a deep recess in the leading edge of the body, clearly intended to add more front-end downforce through the low-speed corners that predominate on American road circuits. At the sides of this aggressive-looking protrusion were the inlet nostrils for air to cool the front brakes and Koni shock absorbers.

Three more cars were built to this amended design, the fourth in the series being sold at the end of June, 1974, to Francisco Mir, for whom it was driven variously by Nestor Garcia-Veiga, Lella Lombardi and John Morton. Heavily modified, by the end of the season it was almost unrecognizable as an Eagle.

Finding no other customers, Dan Gurney decided to field a two-car Formula 5000 team himself. He gained the sponsorship of Jorgensen Steel and signed the experienced Roy Winkelmann as team manager. As drivers Dan signed two youthful Americans: twenty-eight-year-old Brett Lunger, who had done some of the final testing of the new car, and thirty-year-old Elliott Forbes-Robinson II, who, unlike Lunger, had never raced a car of such potency before.

Had there been a concours d'elegance at the first F.5000 race at Mid-Ohio, on June 2, the two Eagles would have won with ease. They were spectacular in their light blue livery with dark blue and red trim. But the vital element of speed was lacking. For AAR, that was unforgivable. AAR Eagles are allowed to break, but they may never be slow. "We've built the fifth-fastest car at Mid-Ohio," mourned Gurney, after Lunger qualified behind four Lola-Chevys. Lack of a spare engine (due to the rush of readying for Indy just days earlier) kept the second Eagle from qualifying. In the Continental Series format of two heat races and a final, Lunger brought home a second-place finish at Mid-Ohio — a happy result for a car that hadn't been run before pre-race practice.

Analysis of the cars' performance at Mid-Ohio convinced the AAR crew that the inboard front brakes didn't offer enough in return for the weight penalty involved, some thirty-five pounds. So the brakes were moved outboard as the workloads of the crewmen — Bobby Boxx, Haff Haffenden and Bert Brown — permitted. In mid-June, Forbes-Robinson placed second in a heat race at Mosport, after a very forceful and spirited drive, but in the final he spun off and out of the picture. Brett Lunger finished third in the final.

The 1974 Jorgensen Eagle team drivers: Brett Lunger (top) and Elliott Forbes-Robinson II (bottom).

Elliott Forbes-Robinson II at Mid-Ohio,
debut of the 1974 Formula 5000 Eagle.

The next three races were an arid patch for the Eagles, thanks to retirements, the thirst for victory being quenched only once, by Brett Lunger's win in a heat at Ontario on September 1. He was knocked out of the final by a crash caused by another driver. His car was so badly damaged that Dan Gurney decided to build an all-new Formula 5000 Eagle for the last two Continental events instead of expending the same effort on extensive repairs. Dan hoped an early appearance by the 1975 model would gain valuable test experience and attract some customers for cars for the new season. At the eleventh hour the SCCA and USAC had worked out a joint sanctioning arrangement for the Continental Series in 1974, allowing drivers and cars from each organization to compete in the other's events. Gurney felt this kind of cooperation was vital to the future growth of auto racing in America, and wanted to be sure that AAR was contributing to this détente with the best cars and drivers it could command.

Design work on the new Formula 5000 Eagle had begun on June 1, just after Indy and just *before* the '74 model raced for the first time! AAR knew that its 1974 F.5000 car was overweight, at about 1,575 pounds with the inboard brakes, and aimed to lighten the new one if possible. They also sought a less costly and simpler car with aerodynamics better suited to U.S. road racing. Composed of an oval-section tower atop a sharp-nosed wedge, its shape was reminiscent of the 1969 Eagle-Santa Ana. Placed at the trailing edge of the wedge, between it and the rear tires, were the two coolant radiators.

Dubbed the Type 755, in a new designation system adopted by AAR with this model, the 1975 F.5000 Eagle was given a simpler mono-coque frame, made possible by its entirely exposed front suspension. This suspension featured exceptionally long and wide-based wishbones, with steeply inclined spring/shock units arranged to give a rising suspension rate with jounce. Tucked deep inside the Melmag wheels, the front brakes were cooled by narrow rectangular-section scoops. The engine bay was left uncovered apart from the tall air scoop mounted atop the ram pipes on the injectors feeding the John Miller Chevrolet engine. Between the engine and the transaxle a spacer was installed, during the 755's development, that extended its wheelbase from the designed 103 inches to 105 inches.

Uncharacteristically for AAR, the Type 755 came to the line for its first race at Laguna Seca on October 13, 1974, with its aluminum skin showing, bereft of paint. Another first for AAR was the company's use of a British driver in a works entry: James Hunt. England's premier Grand Prix driver, Hunt was tapped by Dan to replace Forbes-Robinson in the team because, said Dan, "I wanted to bring in a heavyweight, hopefully to generate sales." He was contacted by Gurney about the assignment at the U.S. Grand Prix and became the first man to push the new car hard during a special test day on October 9. "A great tribute to the men who built the car," wrote Hunt later for *Autoweek*, "was the fact that we did the whole test day and race meeting without any serious problems and very few minor ones."[5]

[5] *Autoweek*, vol 24 (November 16, 1974), p 6.

Hunt and the 755 brought AAR some luck, but not enough for a victory. They placed second in the final at Laguna Seca, while Lunger retired with engine trouble in the 1974 car. Hunt drove the new car again at Riverside, where handling problems slowed him and eventually forced him into a wall and out of the race. In that October 27 race Lunger salvaged a sixth-place finish with a cover over the central nose airfoil of the 1974 Eagle to reduce high-speed drag, and deep scoops in front of the side

An interesting view of Brett Lunger's F.5000 Eagle (left). James Hunt's (spelled "Shunt" on the car) type 755 Eagle at Laguna Seca where it placed second in 1974 (above). *(Overleaf)* He confers with Dan and Roman Slobodynskyj.

radiators to improve cooling. This left Lunger in fifth place in the final Continental Championship point standings, not nearly so high as AAR had hoped.

At one point in the second heat at Riverside *three* AAR-entered Eagles were running virtually nose to tail. Where did the third one come from? Since Bobby Unser had already clinched the USAC Championship, Dan Gurney decided to enter him and the Indy Eagle-Offy in the Riverside contest, for which USAC cars were eligible — though few of them had been successful at road racing. Unser and the big white Eagle were something else again. They qualified second fastest and ran away from the field in the second heat. In the final they leaped into the lead again, chased closely by Andretti's Lola, only to retire with an engine failure provoked by an over-revving incident in practice.

This Riverside race gave a preview of the planned AAR alignment in Formula 5000 for the 1975 season. Gurney picked Bobby Unser as his driver for a full-season challenge in the ten-race F.5000 series in North America. "It will be a new thing for Bobby because most of his experience is in USAC," Dan admitted. "But I hope to be able to transfer some of my road-racing experience to our effort and we expect to be a front-runner." The season did not, unfortunately, come up to Gurney's expectations.

They started seriously enough with the completion of a second Type 755 early in 1975 and the continuation of the 1,500-pound car's development with Bobby Unser as the tester. (By the end of February all but the first of the 1974 cars had been sold.) AAR experimented with two different front suspension systems and two wheel offsets at the front, and fitted cockpit controls that allowed the stiffness of the front and rear anti-roll bars to be changed by the driver during a test or race. The engine oil cooler was moved to the nose, where it drew fresh air from a slot across the very tip. Gary Wheeler supervised the necessary design work, for the economic pinch had forced AAR to lay off the two others who had designed the Type 755, Roman Slobodynskyj and Dick Lindhurst, plus all but the core of their car-building crew.

James Hunt. Below, he models the latest footwear fashion among Grand Prix stars.

With the cancellation of a planned race at Edmonton, the Formula 5000 Championship series still jointly sanctioned by USAC and the SCCA dropped to nine firm events for the '75 season. Each consisted of two sixty-mile heat races that determined the starting order for the main event, the one-hundred-mile final. In the heat races $5,000 was awarded, and according to the result of the final race the rest of the purse, typically $60,000, was distributed and the championship points were alloted. Bobby Unser drove the Chevy-powered Jorgensen-blue Eagle in only two of the nine races and saw precious little of either points or cash.

The series opener was at Pocono International Raceway on June 1, just a week after Indy. Bobby placed third in his heat but the final was swept by the same stormy rains that had helped him in Indiana. Here they sent him spinning twice and dropped him to sixth place at the finish. Then at Mosport two weeks later he was second in the heat race, a promising showing, but retired with suspension trouble after seventeen laps of the forty-lap main event.

For the third event of 1975 Gurney put a newcomer to AAR in the driver's seat of the F.5000 car. This was Vern Schuppan, one of the many Australians who've made good in international racing. He jumped quickly from the Formula Atlantic Championship in 1971 to some Grand Prix rides with B.R.M. in 1972, then to long-distance races and a European F.5000 campaign in 1974 in which he collected two wins and then caught the eye of Dan Gurney in season-end outings in the West Coast races. He showed an ability to qualify fast and lead races that was especially appealing to the intensely competitive Gurney.

Schuppan wasn't able to do much with the Type 755 on his first acquaintance with it at Watkins Glen on July 13. He finished eighth in his heat and seventh, more than a lap back, in the final. At Road America two weeks later he was still not happy with the Eagle's handling, saying it was "okay in the faster corners but in the slow ones it's terrible." In spite of engine difficulties they made some chassis improvements during practice that allowed Schuppan to mount a challenge for fourth place in his heat race that faded, however, when a rear suspension element came adrift. In

Australian-born Vern Schuppan, driver of the 1975 Formula 5000 Jorgensen Eagle.

doing so it damaged a wishbone that couldn't be repaired or replaced in time for the car to race in the main event.

Though he was only ninth fastest in the starting field, Schuppan had a better race at Mid-Ohio on August 10. He was fifth in his heat and fifth again in the final. The AAR team passed up the next event at Road Atlanta so it could prepare to the teeth for the historic Long Beach Grand Prix on the streets of that Southern California city. Dan Gurney had strongly supported this race, driving an Eagle over the roads to check them out and serving as operations vice president for the September 28 event, which was a precursor of a full-fledged Formula 1 Grand Prix race for the West Coast.

Fittingly, Schuppan in the AAR Eagle was the first to drive at speed on the Long Beach course when it was finally completed at 1:05 p.m. on the Friday before the race. Vern was middling fast in qualifying, quick in the first heat with a fourth-place finish, and even quicker with a second-place finish in the final, good for $16,000 in prize money. Granted, both Schuppan and winner (and series champion) Brian Redman benefited from the retirements of three faster runners.

Long Beach was easily the high point of the season for the AAR Formula 5000 campaign. In the subsequent two races Schuppan and the Eagle were all but invisible. At Laguna Seca on October 12 they were seventh in their heat race, suffering from inconsistent handling, and then fell out of the final six miles past the half-way point when a right front suspension wishbone broke. At the very fast Riverside track the report card was equally dismal. They were fifteenth fastest of twenty-nine qualifiers, eighth in their heat and a distant ninth in the main race. Vern tangled with another car and spun in the final, but this had little effect on an already mediocre performance. He closed out the year in eighth place in the Formula 5000 Championship.

This was not the way AAR wanted to end the season. The F.5000 Eagle of 1975 had proved to be, like the Grand Prix Eagle of 1968, unreliable "and worse, not competitive." This, said Dan Gurney, "has been an extremely sobering experience for AAR after so much success in Indy racing. It has only pointed out that 'Dame Fortune' had a lot of influence on our many successes. Our inability to follow on with a similarly successful F.5000 car has been rude to our reputations, has had disruptive effects on about eight different drivers, and has caused the collapse and reorganization of the AAR design staff." With his new staff Dan was hard at work at the end of 1975 on a new kind of Eagle, one designed to be as versatile, in different worlds of racing, as the original 1966 model.

Vern Schuppan in the disappointing 1975 Eagle road-course car.

7 Bicentennial Eagle

If the great she-god Destiny had any compassion in her soul, she surely looked kindly on the plans of her California son, Dan Gurney, for a new All American Eagle racing car in the year of America's Bicentennial celebration. No year offered better prospects for the birth of a new Eagle than 1976.

Yet if the '76 Eagle should prove successful Dan Gurney will not attribute that success to Destiny. He will know that it was hard work and an unwillingness to accept less than perfection that made it what it is. It is this determination to achieve the best possible results in the toughest of the world's racing leagues that keeps Dan Gurney going and accounts for the respect he has won for himself, his company and his nation wherever men speak of speed on wheels.

"There is no race car in the world that is perfect," Dan said recently. "There is always room for betterment, even from race to race, or from qualifying to race day. In my opinion it is a part of winning and an important way to survive. In all my career, I never was fully happy with my car. I was not an easy one to please. I always had a lot of complaints and some ideas how to improve a car. To a large extent I did it because of my own safety," Dan continued. "I felt I had a much better chance of not getting killed in a race car if I familiarized myself with all the mechanical and technical aspects of that car. I can think of quite a few drivers who might still be with us today if they had developed the necessary knowledge and interest to understand a race car so they would have been able to interpret messages about things going wrong before they actually did."

When the head man of the company that makes Eagles holds these views, is it any wonder that Eagle cars are considered to be among the most meticulously crafted, safe and dependable racing cars in the world? Now for 1976 all Dan Gurney had to do was give them blistering speed to boot. He was confident that this could be done.

"We were competitive wherever we went," Dan said about USAC racing in 1975. Thanks to the Indy win, he added, "it was a good year for the racing team." But he realized that others were gnawing away at his Eagle's speed as they refined their newer designs: Foyt with his Coyote and Bignotti with his Wildcat. The car that had revolutionized racing in 1972 was no longer likely to be fast enough in 1976, especially under the new USAC ground rules of better fuel consumption and lower supercharging pressures that placed a greater premium on ultra-low aerodynamic drag.

And then there was the need for a new Eagle for Formula 5000. Close racing and strong sponsor support had helped this championship series grow in stature and popularity in the United States, where it had taken over from the Can-Am series as the premier showcase for road-racing cars and drivers. It had become a series that demanded to be populated by Eagle cars as intensely and successfully as it was in 1968 and 1969. But could they stage a comeback after the poor performances of 1974 and '75? "We've always managed to come back as strong as ever," said Dan Gurney. Then, after a moment's reflection, "I think we'll come back *stronger* than ever!"

The Eagle that carried AAR on the comeback trail was conceived as a dual-purpose car that could serve for both USAC and Formula 5000 competition, much as the original Eagle of a decade earlier had been designed to suit both Indianapolis and Grand Prix racing, with different engines. It wasn't easy for Dan Gurney to get his staff to tear up the designs that had been successful in the past and make a fresh start with new ideas. They were most comfortable with the cars they knew best. When the crew was pared to the bone, however, those remaining at AAR were the ones most willing to experiment. "Under the old setup," Gurney explained, "we didn't have the enthusiasm to come up with a new generation of stuff."

Dan feels his new design staff is the strongest AAR has ever had. Heading it is Gary Wheeler, now an AAR veteran, who began as a specialist in structures and aerodynamics. Backing him up are two new engineers, recent university graduates: John Ward and Ron Hopkins. They've prepared modifications to the 1975 USAC Eagle for Duane 'Pancho' Carter's approval in 1976; if the changes work out they may be marketed by AAR to the owners of existing Eagles, They're planning a Formula 1 Grand Prix version of the all-new Eagle, a car that might again carry the red, white and blue emblem of AAR on tracks around the world.

Testing was scheduled for March, 1976, for the Bicentennial Eagle in its Formula 5000 form, with a Chevrolet engine built by John Miller. "It is our intention," said Dan Gurney, "that the concepts included in the new 5000 car will constitute the basis for an all-new Jorgensen Eagle Indy car. We plan to use a new updated version of the highly successful tur-

Duane 'Pancho' Carter, Jr. (left) is shown with Earle M. Jorgensen, Chairman of the Board, Jorgensen Steel Co., and Dan Gurney.

bocharged Drake engine." This engine, being developed jointly by AAR and Drake Engineering, has a narrower valve angle for a more compact, efficient combustion chamber.

So it could be adapted to both types of engines, and even to a Formula 1 three-liter power unit, the new car's chassis has a tubular structure from the firewall back and a monocoque shell from there forward. For the sake of simplicity and lightness its coil/shock suspension assemblies and its disc brakes are placed outboard at all wheels.

"We're trying to make a little bit smaller hole in the air," said Gurney of the design philosophy behind the new Eagle. This was done by narrowing the track, in proportion to the wheelbase, and by covering the front of the car with a wide 'sports car' nose that lets air flow more smoothly over the exposed wheels and the rest of the body. The Eagle is shaped to extract more aerodynamic downforce from the body itself and less from wings, which can exact a heavy penalty in drag for the downforce they provide. It's an approach that should pay dividends on the long straights at Indy, at Ontario and on America's road courses.

The urge and desire to try a new form for the Eagle is typical of Dan Gurney's ever-questing intellect. His restless curiosity about the world of motor vehicles has caused AAR to diversify in many ways. Its short-lived liaison with Plymouth included the preparation and racing of Barracudas in the Trans-Am series in 1970. AAR has built and tested racing motorcycles, a personal passion of Dan's. It has planned completely new types of engines, including a sleeve-valve design aimed at low emissions and better economy. There'll always be something novel brewing in the back rooms of that building on a corner lot in Santa Ana.

Above all, in its first decade All American Racers has justly been identified with the designing, building and racing of cars of outstanding grace, quality and speed. How aptly they were named Eagles! Under Gurney's guidance AAR has never had to build down to its markets, and one hopes it never will. Its challenge has not been to make the most racing cars, but the best and the fastest. AAR has done this with skill and dedication, greatly honoring thereby the nation that is part of the company name.

Jerry Eisert, veteran AAR team member and chief mechanic for Duane Carter, Jr.'s 1976 Jorgensen Eagle in USAC competition.

On the very short honor roll of racing cars that have won both Grand Prix races and the Indianapolis 500 there are only two American names: Duesenberg and Eagle. That puts the sharp-beaked cars from California in select and suitable company. Fred and Augie Duesenberg would have been proud of Gurney's Eagles.

Pancho Carter with Dan. In 1974 Carter was Indy 500 rookie of the year and national sprint car champion. In 1975 he finished fourth at Indy.

Appendix A
Eagle Specifications

	1966 FORMULA 1	1968 FORMULA 1	1966 USAC/INDY	1968 USAC/INDY	1968 FORMULA A	1969 USAC/INDY	1970 USAC/INDY	1972 USAC/INDY	1973 USAC/INDY	1974 FORMULA 5000	1975 FORMULA 5000
Wheelbase (ins.)	96.5	96.5	96.5	96.3	96.3	99.9	96.5	102	102	102.4	105
Front Track	61.0	58.0	61.0	58.0	56.0	57.0	59.0	63.0	65.0	63.0	63.0
Rear Track	61.0	56.0	61.0	58.0	52.0	55.6	57.5	58.0	61.0	62.0	62.0
Length	162	164	162	150	150	167	155	180	180	178	175
Width	73	70	73	68	68	70	71	74	75	79	79
Height	35.5	35.5	36	34	34	34	35	32	38	46.5	46
Weight (lbs.)	1,240	1,190	1,350	1,380	1,470	1,440	1,550	1,540	1,500	1,575	1,500
Fuel Capy. (U.S. gals.)	65	58	75	72	30	75	75	75	75	30	30
Front Wheels	15 x 8.5	15 x 10	15 x 8.5	15 x 8.5	15 x 11	15 x 10	15 x 10	15 x 10	15 x 10	13 x 11	13 x 11
Rear Wheels	15 x 9.5	15 x 14	15 x 9.5	15 x 9.5	15 x 16	15 x 14	15 x 14	15 x 14	15 x 14	15 x 17	15 x 17
Engine	CLIMAX	WESLAKE	FORD	GURNEY	CHEV	GURNEY	DRAKE	DRAKE	DRAKE	CHEV	CHEV
Cylinders	4	V-12	V-8	V-8	V-8	V-8	4	4	4	V-8	V-8
Bore (mm)	96.0	72.8	95.5	101.9	101.6	104.4	108.7	111.3	111.3	102.1	104.9
Stroke	95.0	60.0	72.9	76.2	76.2	76.2	69.9	67.3	67.3	76.2	72.0
Displacement (cc)	2751	2997	4177	4967	4942	5218	2593	2617	2617	4991	4975
Power (bhp)	255	390	530	543	450	580	800	900	950	510	n.a.
@ RPM	7200	10,000	8800	7800	7500	7600	9000	9000	9000	8000	n.a.

Appendix B
Major Successes Achieved by AAR Teams

1965

| First: Joe Leonard | Milwaukee 150 | USAC oval | Indy Shrike |

(Pole position: Dan Gurney at the Milwaukee 150.)

1966

| First: Jerry Grant | Bridgehampton USRRC | SCCA road race | Lola Group 7 |
| First: Dan Gurney | Bridgehampton Can-Am | SCCA road race | Lola Group 7 |

1967

First: Dan Gurney	Race of Champions	road race	Eagle F-1
First: Dan Gurney	Grand Prix of Belgium	road race	Eagle F-1
First: Dan Gurney	Rex Mays 300	USAC road race	Indy Eagle

(Dan Gurney was fastest qualifier at Brands Hatch, Spa, Nurburgring, Can-Am Times Grand Prix Riverside and Rex Mays Riverside; he was front-row qualifier for the Indy 500.)

1968

First: Dan Gurney	Mosport 200	USAC road race	Indy Eagle
First: Dan Gurney	Rex Mays 300	USAC road race	Indy Eagle
Second: Dan Gurney	Indianapolis 500	USAC oval	Indy Eagle
Fourth: Denis Hulme	Indianapolis 500	USAC oval	Indy Eagle

1969

First: Dan Gurney	Indy Raceway Park 100	USAC road race	Indy Eagle
First: Dan Gurney	Donnybrooke 100	USAC road race	Indy Eagle
Second: Dan Gurney	Indianapolis 500	USAC oval	Indy Eagle
Second: Dan Gurney	Castle Rock 150	USAC road race	Indy Eagle
Third: Dan Gurney	Rex Mays 300	USAC road race	Indy Eagle

(Dan Gurney was the fastest qualifier at all four road races plus the Dan Gurney 200 at Kent Raceway, Seattle.)

1970

First: Dan Gurney	Sears Point	USAC road race	Indy Eagle
First: Swede Savage	Phoenix 150	USAC oval	Indy Eagle
Third: Dan Gurney	Indianapolis 500	USAC oval	Indy Eagle

(Dan was the fastest qualifier at Sears Point and front-row qualifier at the California 500.)

1971

| First: Bobby Unser | Milwaukee 200 | USAC oval | Indy Eagle |
| First: Bobby Unser | Trenton 300 | USAC oval | Indy Eagle |

1972

First: Bobby Unser	Phoenix 150	USAC oval	Indy Eagle
First: Bobby Unser	Milwaukee 150	USAC oval	Indy Eagle
First: Bobby Unser	Trenton 300	USAC oval	Indy Eagle
First: Bobby Unser	Phoenix 200	USAC oval	Indy Eagle

(Eight track records set. Eight pole positions—including pole position at the Indy 500, Pocono 500 and California 500 races—by Bobby Unser and Jerry Grant. World speed record on a closed circuit—Ontario—by Bobby Unser in an Indy Eagle.)

1973

First: Bobby Unser	Milwaukee 150	USAC oval	Indy Eagle
Second: Bobby Unser	Trenton 200	USAC oval	Indy Eagle

1974

First: Bobby Unser	California 500	USAC oval	Indy Eagle
First: Bobby Unser	Trenton 200	USAC oval	Indy Eagle
First: Bobby Unser	Trenton 300	USAC oval	Indy Eagle
First: Bobby Unser	Michigan 200	USAC oval	Indy Eagle
Second: Bobby Unser	Indianapolis 500	USAC oval	Indy Eagle
Second: Bobby Unser	Phoenix 150	USAC oval	Indy Eagle
Second: Bobby Unser	Phoenix 150	USAC oval	Indy Eagle
Second: Brett Lunger	Mid-Ohio	USAC/SCCA road race	F. 5000 Eagle

1975

First: Bobby Unser	Indianapolis 500	USAC oval	Indy Eagle
Second: Bobby Unser	California 500	USAC oval	Indy Eagle
Second: Bobby Unser	Milwaukee 150	USAC oval	Indy Eagle
Second: Vern Schuppan	Long Beach Grand Prix	USAC oval	F. 5000 Eagle

---

Appendix C
Major Successes Achieved by AAR Customers

1966

First: Roger McCluskey	Langhorne 150	USAC oval	Indy Eagle

1967

First: Lloyd Ruby	Langhorne 150	USAC oval	Indy Eagle
First: Lloyd Ruby	Phoenix 150	USAC oval	Indy Eagle
First: Bobby Unser	Mosport 100	USAC road race	Indy Eagle
First: Bobby Unser	Mosport	USAC road race	Indy Eagle
First: Gordon Johncock	Hanford 200	USAC road race	Indy Eagle

(Denis Hulme, fourth in the Indy 500, was Rookie of the Year.)

1968

First: Bobby Unser	*National Championship*	USAC	Indy Eagle
First: Dr. Lou Sell	*Grand Prix Championship*	SCCA	F. A Eagle
First: Bobby Unser	Indianapolis 500	USAC oval	Indy Eagle
First: Bobby Unser	Las Vegas 150	USAC road race	Indy Eagle
First: Bobby Unser	Trenton 150	USAC oval	Indy Eagle
First: Bobby Unser	Phoenix 150	USAC oval	Indy Eagle
First: Gordon Johncock	Hanford 200	USAC road race	Indy Eagle
First: Dr. Lou Sell	Castle Rock	SCCA road race	F. A Eagle
First: Dr. Lou Sell	War Bonnet Park	SCCA road race	F. A Eagle
First: Dr. Lou Sell	Thompson	SCCA road race	F. A Eagle
First: Dr. Lou Sell	Mosport	SCCA road race	F. A Eagle
First: Dr. Lou Sell	Laguna Seca	SCCA road race	F. A Eagle
First: George Wintersteen	Lime Rock	SCCA road race	F. A Eagle
First: George Wintersteen	Donnybrooke	SCCA road race	F. A Eagle

1969

First: Tony Adamowicz	*Continental Championship*	SCCA	F. A Eagle
First: Tony Adamowicz	Seattle Raceway Park	SCCA road race	F. A Eagle
First: Tony Adamowicz	Elkhart Lake	SCCA road race	F. A Eagle
First: John Cannon	Riverside	SCCA road race	F. A Eagle
First: Sam Posey	Laguna Seca	SCCA road race	F. A Eagle
First: John Cannon	Sears Point	SCCA road race	F. A Eagle
First: John Cannon	Mosport	SCCA road race	F. A Eagle

1972

Second: Billy Vukovich	*National Championship*	USAC	Indy Eagle

(Mike Hiss, Rookie of the Year, at Indianapolis 500.)

1973

First: Gordon Johncock	Indianapolis 500	USAC oval	Indy Eagle
First: Wally Dallenbach	Milwaukee 200	USAC oval	Indy Eagle
First: Wally Dallenbach	Ontario 100	USAC oval	Indy Eagle
First: Wally Dallenbach	California 500	USAC oval	Indy Eagle
First: Billy Vukovich	Michigan 126	USAC oval	Indy Eagle
First: Gordon Johncock	Trenton 200	USAC oval	Indy Eagle
First: Gordon Johncock	Arizona 150	USAC oval	Indy Eagle
Second: Billy Vukovich	Indianapolis 500	USAC oval	Indy Eagle

1974

First: Mike Mosley	Phoenix 150	USAC oval	Indy Eagle

1975

First: Mike Mosley	Milwaukee 200	USAC oval	Indy Eagle
First: Wally Dallenbach	Ontario 100	USAC oval	Indy Eagle

Appendix D
Production of Eagle Cars

Grand Prix Eagles:

Eagle-Climax	1
Eagle-Weslake	3
Total	**4**

Formula A / 5000 Eagles:

1968 model	6
1969 model	8
1974 model	4
1975 model	1
1976 model	1
Total	**20**

Indianapolis / USAC Eagles:

1966 model	6
1967 model	6
1968 model	8
1969 model (Santa Ana)	4
1970 model	6
1971 model	2
1972 model	28
1973 model	6
1974 model	15
Total	**81**

Grand Total (March, 1976):   *105*

Photograph Credits

Pete Biro: 23 both, 29, 40 bottom, 44, 72, 78, 79, 101, 102, 104, 106-107, 109, 113 both, 114, 116, 117, 118-119, 120 both, 122, 123, 127, 128

Kenneth Coles: 97, 100 top left

Bibliography

Calvin, Jean. *Those Incredible Indy Cars.* New York: Sports Car Press, 1973.

Clymer, Floyd. *Indianapolis 500 Mile Race Yearbook.* Los Angeles: Clymer, 1965, 1966, 1967, 1968.

Davidson, Donald. *Indianapolis 500 Annual.* Speedway, Indiana: Davidson, 1974.

Donohue, Mark, and Paul Van Valkenburgh. *The Unfair Advantage.* New York: Dodd, Mead & Company, 1975.

Heintzelman, Bob. *Racing Scene Indianapolis 500.* Indianapolis: Motor Publications, 1971.

Hungness, Carl. *The Indianapolis 500 Yearbook.* Speedway, Indiana: Carl Hungness and Associates, 1973, 1974, 1975.

Levine, Leo. *Ford: The Dust and the Glory.* New York: Macmillan, Inc., 1968.

Ludvigsen, Karl. *Group 7.* New York: World, 1971.

Manso, Peter. *Vrooom!!* New York: Funk & Wagnalls, 1969.

Terry, Len, and Alan Baker. *Racing Car Design and Development.* Cambridge, Massachusetts: Robert Bentley, 1973.

Also consulted were such periodicals as *Motor, Autocar, Road & Track, Motoring News, Autoweek, Car and Driver, Motor Trend, National Speed Sport News, Auto Topics, Car Life, Auto Italiana, Automobil Revue, Motor Sport, AAR Eagle Club News Letter* and *Jorgensen Eagle Racing Team Newsletter.*

Index